And
Sarah
Laughed

And Sarah Laughed

The Status of Woman in the Old Testament

by John H. Otwell

The Westminster Press
Philadelphia

Unless otherwise indicated, Scripture quotations are from the Revised Standard Version of The Holy Bible, Old Testament Section, Copyright 1952; New Testament Section, First Edition, Copyright 1946; New Testament Section, Second Edition, © 1972 by the Division of Christian Education of the National Council of the Churches of Christ in the U.S.A. Used by permission.

Published by The Westminster Press®
Philadelphia, Pennsylvania

PRINTED IN THE UNITED STATES OF AMERICA

9   8   7   6   5   4   3

Library of Congress Cataloging in Publication Data

Otwell, John H
   And Sarah laughed.

   Bibliography: p.
   Includes index.
   1. Woman (Theology)—Biblical teaching. 2. Bible.
O.T.—Criticism, interpretation, etc. I. Title.
BS1199.W7088   296.3'87'83412   76–54671
ISBN 0–664–24126–3

Contents

Preface

This book presents a new view of the status of woman in the Old Testament. The data and the lines of reasoning upon which the view rests are given. Scholars in general have believed that woman had a low status in ancient Israel, and only a few titles can be cited in support of the conclusions advocated here. Except for the many references to the Old Testament, documentation has been kept to a minimum. Unless otherwise noted, the second edition of the Revised Standard Version is used throughout. Readers unfamiliar with technical Old Testament studies will find helpful the notes and articles provided in *The New Oxford Annotated Bible, The Revised Standard Version*, edited by Herbert G. May and Bruce M. Metzger, 2d ed. (Oxford University Press, 1973).

I could not have written AND SARAH LAUGHED without help. The trustees of the Pacific School of Religion made the necessary time available by granting a sabbatical leave. Four students—Roberta Cook, Grace Drake, Elizabeth Ellenburg, and Sheila Fabricant—made substantive contributions in research papers presented in classes. Other students and faculty colleagues contributed interest and support.

AND SARAH LAUGHED is dedicated to Marion Grace Otwell, my wife. She has contributed to it in many ways, among them by her encouragement and careful editorial reading.

J.H.O.

Introduction

The title for this examination of the status of woman in the Old Testament has been taken from Gen., ch. 18. Abraham, sitting in front of his tent in the heat of the day, has visitors. While they wash off the dust of their journey and rest under a tree, he slaughters a calf and Sarah prepares "a morsel of bread." After the meal, the talk turns first to the promise of a son to Abraham and Sarah, then to the fate of Sodom and Gomorrah. Both are fitting subjects, because the guests turn out to be God.

The aging Sarah responds to the promise of a son with laughter. Thereupon,

> The LORD said to Abraham, "Why did Sarah laugh, and say, 'Shall I indeed bear a child, now that I am old?' Is anything too hard for the LORD? At the appointed time I will return to you, in the spring, and Sarah shall have a son." But Sarah denied, saying, "I did not laugh"; for she was afraid. He said, "No, but you did laugh." (Gen. 18:13–15)

Sarah's conduct is so much at odds with the traditional picture of the ancient Israelite woman as a self-effacing household slave that the phrase "and Sarah laughed" has become the title for this reexamination of the status of woman in the Old Testament.

Writers on the Old Testament with but few exceptions have stressed the subordination of daughter and wife to father and husband. Earle Bennett Cross wrote:

> Throughout most of the history of the Hebrew people, men have been the more prominent sex. The patronymic idea has prevailed. A few exceptions such as Deborah and Queen Athaliah only serve to emphasize the secondary position which was the lot of most of their sex.[1]

Roland de Vaux described the husband as "master" of the wife:

> In the normal type of Israelite marriage the husband is the "master," the *ba'al* of his wife. The father had absolute authority over his children, even over his married sons if they lived with him, and over their wives. In early times this authority included even the power over life and death; thus Judah condemned to death his daughter-in-law Tamar when she was accused of misconduct.[2]

According to Anthony Phillips, a specialist in Biblical law,

> only free adult males had legal status in ancient Israel, and so the right to appear before the elders in court. All other persons whether women, children or slaves, were in effect regarded as the personal property of the heads of the household.[3]

There have been dissenting voices. Ismar J. Peritz seems to have demonstrated as long ago as 1898 that the religion of the Old Testament was not exclusively a male activity,[4] a conclusion supported by a recent doctoral dissertation by Clarence Vos.[5] Elizabeth Mary Mac-Donald proved that women throughout the ancient Near East had more rights and a higher status than has often been asserted.[6] Millar Burrows argued convincingly that the bride-purchase hypothesis did not describe correctly the significance of gifts exchanged at the time of marriage.[7] Recently, Phyllis Trible has suggested that it was the intention of the authors of the Old Testament to further "salvation for both women and men," not to promote the patriarchalism of ancient Israelite culture.[8] Other titles continue to appear.[9]

A basic trait of all scientific study is the constant review of conclusions drawn from evidence by a reexamination of that evidence. This work is the result of such a reexamination. It will submit for judgment conclusions substantially different from the majority of scholarly views of the status of the ancient Israelite woman, and it will present the evidence upon which its conclusions are based.

That evidence is taken primarily from the Jewish and Protestant canons of the Old Testament. These are identical in content, although the order of the books differs (as does the versification at times). Books present in the Roman Catholic canon but lacking in the Jewish-Protestant canon and post-canonical Jewish writings may reflect a change in the status of woman. This question is far too complex to be examined here. Within the canon as just defined, the evidence is restricted primarily to those passages which mention a woman. Each passage was studied individually, using the methods of Biblical criticism.[10] A topical outline finally emerged.

Archaeologists have provided a second, extensive body of evidence. In part, the evidence is the housewares and personal belongings used by ancient Israelite women. In part, it is in the form of legal, mythological, and commercial texts from the ancient Near East. These sources will be introduced when they become helpful. They will not be used, however, to establish a pattern of meaning to which the evidence in the Old Testament will be expected to conform.

The Old Testament was written over many centuries. Even if we reject the traditional dates given the books of

Scripture, we have to face the possibility that a passage may fall anywhere between about 1200 B.C. (the date often assigned Judg., ch. 5) and 175 B.C. (the date often given much of The Book of Daniel). Thus we are dealing with writings composed across a thousand years. If we reflect on the changes in beliefs, customs, technology, government, and language that have occurred in Great Britain since 1066, the possibility that there were changes in Israelite customs and attitudes over a millennium becomes clear. Ancient civilizations appear to have altered slowly, but a thousand years is too long a time in human history for there to have been no change.

Dating passages is difficult and often controversial. I accept historical criticism, one aspect of Biblical criticism, and the dates it provides, rather than the dates recorded in ancient, extra-Biblical tradition. Historical criticism, however, does not provide a precise date for every passage, nor are historical critics always agreed upon the dates they do assign. Dating here will be primarily a matter of relative chronology. The "before or after" sequence will represent either my understanding of scholarly consensus or the conclusion that seems most likely to me. The conclusions of Otto Eissfeldt will often be accepted.[11] The assignment of dates will often be indicated by nothing more than the order in which passages are discussed. Where a precise date is possible and is relevant, it will be stated.

The author shares the belief that the Bible should be read as a human document. We should bring to bear upon our study of the Bible all the resources we normally use in the study of other human documents. Nonetheless, God is the center of the Old Testament, whether it be taken on its own terms or as part of the canon of a community of faith. We have failed seriously to study the Old Testament if we disregard what it clearly presents as its own center—Israel's statements about its relationships with God. Nor have we addressed ourselves to it as canonical if we have not found Israel's statements to be uniquely authoritative for us.

As the material that has gone into this study accumulated, it became clear that the God-centeredness of the Old Testament, rather than a sociological structure derived from anthropology, provides the means by which the information available becomes an intelligible unity. This is the reason that this study of the status of woman in the Old Testament is also the Old Testament doctrine of woman.

The sheer mass of the Old Testament passages in which women appear is misleading. As numerous as such passages are, their total still is only a small part of the whole of the Old Testament. Three books—Obadiah, Habakkuk, and Haggai—contain no references to women! We must begin this study with the recognition that the male dominates the Old Testament statistically. This will not be documented here, although it obviously is important for the status of woman in the Old Testament that men are mentioned there more often than are women.

The subtitle of this work is "The Status of Woman in the Old Testament." Status is defined as relative standing. The basic groups within which relative standing are defined are the family and the community. These are the fundamental divisions of AND SARAH LAUGHED. Within the family, the status of woman can be defined in relationship to parents (especially the father) and husband, siblings, and children. In the community as a whole, a woman's standing may be described in terms of her relationships to males and to other women. Because of the theocentricity of the Old Testament, the relationship of the woman to God is the final arbiter of her status.

CHAPTER 1

The Creation of Woman

The Old Testament opens with a relatively late Priestly version of a creation story widely known throughout the ancient Near East. Its description of the creation of man and woman is reported in these words:

> Then God said, "Let us make man in our image, after our likeness; and let them have dominion over the fish of the sea, and over the birds of the air, and over the cattle, and over all the earth, and over every creeping thing that creeps upon the earth." So God created man in his own image, in the image of God he created him; male and female he created them. (Gen. 1:26f.)[12]

A description of the creation of the human race is not the primary purpose of Gen., ch. 1, since the climax of the narrative tells of the establishment of the Sabbath.

Nonetheless, three things are said about woman in Gen. 1:26f. There is no hint that woman had a subordinate status in the description of her creation. Humanity is created male and female. One sex is not elevated above the other, even though both together are placed over all other forms of life. Furthermore, sexuality is a fundamental part of the creation. There is no suggestion that it is evil, or that one of the two sexes is evil because of gender. Such motifs emerge in later Judaism, but they find no justification here.

Finally, Gen. 1:26f. describes man and woman as having been created in the image and in the likeness of God. Because we believe that any physical representation of God is impossible, we assume that the image and the likeness of God is intangible, perhaps humanity's capacity to create and to make moral judgments. It is probable, however, that the Priestly writer had a more literal, physical likeness in mind.[13] The significance of the divine likeness may be found in the authority given humanity over the rest of the creation (v. 28). Female and male share this rule since both were created in the image of God.

Gen. 5:1f. is an echo of Gen. 1:26f.

Gen. 2:4b to 3:24 is widely held to be a second creation narrative. It differs from Gen. 1:1 to 2:4a in vocabulary, the order in which events occur, the dramatic thrust of the narrative, the climax, and the lack of any significant parallel in non-Biblical narratives. Gen. 2:4b to 3:24 is usually assigned to the Yahwist source (called J), the oldest of the strands now woven together to make up the first five books of the Old Testament. It therefore is dated some centuries earlier than Gen., ch. 1.

The creation of woman is described in ch. 2:18–24:

> Then the LORD God said, "It is not good that the man should be alone; I will make him a helper fit for him." So out of the ground the LORD God formed every beast of the field and every bird of the air, and brought them to the man to see what he would call them; and whatever the man called every living creature, that was its name. The man gave names to all cattle, and to the birds of the air, and to every beast of the field; but for the man there was not found a helper fit for him. So the LORD God caused a deep sleep to fall upon the man, and while he slept took one of his ribs and closed up its place with flesh; and the rib which the LORD God had taken from the man he made into a woman and

brought her to the man. Then the man said,
"This at last is bone of my bones
and flesh of my flesh;
she shall be called Woman *('ishshah),*
because she was taken out of Man *('ish)."*
Therefore a man leaves his father and his mother and
cleaves to his wife, and they become one flesh.

A curse is put on Eve later in the story after she and
Adam had disobeyed a divine command:

I will greatly multiply your pain in childbearing;
in pain you shall bring forth children,
yet your desire shall be for your husband,
and he shall rule over you.

(Ch. 3:16)

These verses have provided the primary Old Testament
basis for the depreciation of woman.

It has been claimed that Eve was inferior to Adam
because she had been created as his helpmeet (ch. 2:18).
It is difficult to see how the Hebrew word translated as
helpmeet *('ezer)* could have conveyed inferiority to an
ancient Israelite. It is taken from a verb meaning "to
help." As a noun, it refers to the one giving help twelve
times in the Old Testament (two of them here, vs. 18,
20). The *'ezer* is God, the helper of Israel, in Ex. 18:4;
Deut. 33:7, 26; Ps. 33:20; 70:5; 115:9, 10, 11. Thus *'ezer*
clearly does not denote inferiority!

Eve also has been alleged to be subordinate to Adam
because she is said to have been created from his rib. I
know of no parallel to this and therefore can neither
confirm nor deny that this feature of the story imputes
inferiority to woman.

Adam is reported to have named the woman twice
(chs. 2:23 and 3:20). This is widely understood to be an
exercise of authority over Eve. Gerhard von Rad wrote,
"Let us remind ourselves once more that name-giving in

the ancient Orient was primarily an exercise of sovereignty, of command."[14] Later, in another context, we
will see that mothers name children more often than do
fathers in the Old Testament narratives, yet scholars
have not taken this as evidence that mothers exercised
more authority within the family than did fathers. There
are instances when name-giving expressed a relationship
of authority (as in the naming of a captured city in II Sam.
12:27f.), but there is no justification for seeing an exercise of authority in every act of naming. The naming of
Eve in Gen. 2:23 becomes the occasion for a statement
of a union of husband and wife in which the husband
leaves his own parents (v. 24). This is the meaning given
the act by the author of the story.

The curse on Eve in Gen. 3:16 contains lines that need
careful study:

> yet your desire shall be for your husband,
> and he shall rule over you.

In the structure of Hebrew poetry, the second half of a
line (which appears as the second line in an English
translation) is related closely in content to the first half.
Thus "in pain you shall bring forth children" duplicates
"your pain in childbearing." We may expect, therefore,
that "and he shall rule over you" parallels "your desire
shall be for your husband." Thus the husband's rule
would seem to lie either in the wife's need for her husband because of her desire to have children, or in the
strength of his sexual attraction for her.[15] This is not an
abstract statement of the subordination of the woman to
the man in all relationships, and it also says nothing
about the power of the woman over the man.

Job 31:13–15 contains the only other reference in the
Old Testament to the creation of woman:

If I have rejected the cause of my manservant or my
   maidservant,
when they brought a complaint against me;
what then shall I do when God rises up?
   When he makes inquiry, what shall I answer him?
Did not he who made me in the womb make him?
And did not one fashion us in the womb?

A masculine personal pronoun in Hebrew legal prose can refer to antecedents that are both female and male. So also here. The series of rhetorical questions with which this passage closes applies as much to the maidservant as to the manservant. The sexes are equal in this description of the creation of man and woman.

We have looked at Gen. 1:26f. (ch. 5:1f.); 2:18–24; 3:16; and Job 31:13–15 for information on the status of woman as created by God. If we were to classify these passages according to a modern doctrine of creation, we might say that Gen. 1:26f. (ch. 5:1f.) describes creation *ex nihilo* and that Job 31:13–15 deals with continuing creation. In both of these forms of creation, man and woman are equal.

The narrative in Gen. 2:18–24 and ch. 3:16 fits neither of these contemporary doctrines of creation. The story limits its concern to the creation of life and the continuation of life in a world different from what it was created originally to be. The picture of the status of woman that we gain from the Genesis narrative is less clear. While there seems far less reason to cite the story in support of an inferior position for woman than is widely believed to be the case, there does seem to be present a declaration that woman is sexually dependent upon her husband.

CHAPTER 2

Sexual Attraction

I

Humanity was created female and male and was commanded to "be fruitful and multiply" (Gen. 1:27f.), according to the Priestly writer. This means, among other things, that sexuality, the difference between female and male and the physical attraction of each for the other, was believed to be an essential part of the nature of persons as created by God. Sexuality was not evil, and neither sex could be condemned for being attractive to, or for being attracted by, the other.

We always need to be cautious about drawing far-reaching conclusions on the basis of slight evidence. This is especially true when the conclusion conforms to our standards, expectations, or conduct; for in such circumstances we run the risk of doing nothing more than confirming our preconceptions by a proof text or two. This is the danger we now confront. We live in the midst of a readjustment of sexual mores during which the reticence of a former generation has given way to an often strident, forced sexuality.

Is physical attraction between the sexes actually regarded as normal and right throughout the Old Testament? That is the conclusion we have already stated
about the Priestly writer's attitude toward sexuality, but
this seems to agree so much with the temper of our age
that we need to view it with wariness. The task of this
chapter is to test our statements about Gen. 1:27f. and
to see whether the same conclusion applies to the rest of
the Old Testament.

II

The physical attractiveness of woman for man is frequently expressed throughout the Old Testament. Evidence can be found in the stories used by the Yahwist to
create his national epic, in the narrative of the succession
to David's throne, and in late wisdom literature.

The skill with which the Yahwist has presented the
history of his people from its beginnings to the emergence of the monarchy has always aroused the admira-
tion of students of the Old Testament. The narrative is
realistic and vivid, never sanctimonious; and the matter-
of-factness with which it states the attraction of woman
for man is a part of that strength.

The Yahwist wrote, "When men began to multiply on
the face of the ground, and daughters were born to them,
the sons of God saw that the daughters of men were fair;
and they took to wife such of them as they chose" (Gen.
6:1f.). If gods found women beautiful, would not mere
men also?

In his contribution to the saga of Abram, the ancestor
of all Israel, the Yahwist told a story that puts Abram in
a curious light. Abram moved into Egypt because of a
famine in Palestine, saying to Sarai:

I know that you are a woman beautiful to behold; and when
the Egyptians see you, they will say, "This is his wife"; then
they will kill me, but they will let you live. Say you are my
sister, that it may go well with me because of you, and that
my life may be spared on your account. (Gen. 12:11–13)

Abram's estimate of the effect of his wife's beauty proved
to be correct. Sarai was taken into Pharaoh's harem, and
Abram prospered because of her. The trick was discovered when the Lord sent plagues against Pharaoh. The
king protested the deception in words which still arouse
a sympathetic response: "What is this you have done to
me? Why did you not tell me that she was your wife? Why
did you say, 'She is my sister,' so that I took her for my
wife? Now then, here is your wife, take her, and be gone"
(Gen. 12:18f.). No reverence for Abram can conceal Pharaoh's threefold loss. He enriched Abram under false
pretenses, his household suffered a plague because of his
inadvertent sin, and he lost the beauty whose charms
were the cause of the entire caper. Nothing is said about
Sarai's reaction to her sudden changes in station in life!

Only once did the Yahwist detail any of the feminine
charms of which he clearly was so well aware. He wrote
of the sisters whom Jacob married, "Leah's eyes were
weak, but Rachel was beautiful and lovely" (Gen. 29:17).
Does this mean that Rachel was lovely because she had
strong eyes?

The story of David's family troubles in II Samuel is
held by some scholars to be part of one of the oldest
examples of true history writing. Three times important
parts of this royal history depend upon the attractiveness
of a woman. The first is reported in these words: "It
happened, late one afternoon, when David arose from
his couch and was walking upon the roof of the king's
house, that he saw from the roof a woman bathing; and
the woman was very beautiful" (II Sam. 11:2). The
woman was Bathsheba, the wife of Uriah, a Hittite serv-

ing in the field with David's army. David had her brought to the palace and committed adultery with her so that she conceived. The adultery set in motion a train of events which began with the murder of Uriah, a prophet's condemnation of David, and the death of the child born to the illicit union. David and Bathsheba married after the death of Uriah, and their second child was Solomon.

The second stage of David's family troubles reported the elimination of two of his sons from the succession to the throne through death. The first, Amnon, was killed by his half brother Absalom because Amnon had raped Tamar, Absalom's sister. Absalom in turn was killed during a revolt he launched later against David.

The report of the rape of Tamar opens:

> Now Absalom, David's son, had a beautiful sister, whose name was Tamar; and after a time Amnon, David's son, loved her. And Amnon was so tormented that he made himself ill because of his sister Tamar; for she was a virgin, and it seemed impossible to Amnon to do anything to her. (II Sam. 13:1f.)

Eventually Amnon feigned illness and asked Tamar to wait on him. When she did, he assaulted her. Then he had her driven from his house. David refused to punish the crime, possibly because of his crime against Uriah; and Absalom acted on his sister's behalf, first killing his half brother and then leading a revolt against the king who had refused to execute justice on behalf of Tamar.

The history of David's reign extending from his adultery with Bathsheba to the coronation of Solomon is now called the Succession Document. Its final chapter tells of the rise of Solomon to the throne and of his consolidation of his power. This also opens with an incident in which the beauty of a woman is an essential element:

> Now King David was old and advanced in years; and although they covered him with clothes, he could not get

warm. Therefore his servants said to him, "Let a young
maiden be sought for my lord the king, and let her wait upon
the king, and be his nurse; let her lie in your bosom, that my
lord the king may be warm." So they sought for a beautiful
maiden throughout all the territory of Israel, and found
Abishag the Shunammite, and brought her to the king. The
maiden was very beautiful; and she became the king's nurse
and ministered to him; but the king knew her not. (I Kings
1:1–4)

The statement is quite matter-of-fact. David proved that
he could no longer reign when he was unable to respond
to the charms of the latest addition to the harem.

The response of David and Amnon to feminine beauty
plays a decisive role throughout the candid narrative of
the Succession Document; yet neither David nor Amnon
(nor Bathsheba nor Tamar) was condemned because of
this. David was condemned for adultery and murder.
Amnon was condemned because he raped Tamar and
then refused to marry her (II Sam. 13:11–17). But both
were condemned for crimes, not for being attracted by
the beauty of a woman.

The attraction of woman for man appears in an aside
in Ecclesiastes, a late wisdom writing, according to one
translation of an obscure text. In his recital of the various
ways in which he had tried vainly to find satisfaction in
life, the author wrote, "I also gathered for myself silver
and gold and the treasure of kings and provinces; I got
singers, both men and women, and many concubines,
man's delight" (Eccl. 2:8).[16] If this be the correct translation, we can assume that the author felt himself to be
alluding to something of universal knowledge and acceptance.

III

Descriptions of the attractiveness of the female for the male in the Old Testament can be matched by equally forthright statements of the attraction of the male for the female.

We have already discussed one of these, the curse on Eve in Gen. 3:16. Her desire for her husband will be stronger than her fear of the pain (and risk) of childbirth. The history of the reign of David, which made such use of the appeal of woman's beauty for man, also employed the strength of the male's attraction for the female in its description of the conflict between Saul and David. The relationship between the two men is troubled by David's prowess in battle, a threat to a king whose hold on his throne depended upon his superiority in combat. The description of one of Saul's attempts to neutralize David opens:

> Now Saul's daughter Michal loved David; and they told Saul, and the thing pleased him. Saul thought, "Let me give her to him, that she may be a snare for him, and that the hand of the Philistines may be against him." (I Sam. 18:20f.)

So Saul offered Michal to David in marriage in return for proof that David had killed one hundred Philistines.

The attraction of the man for the woman is described most fully in verses spoken by the maiden in the rhapsodic dialogue between bride and groom in The Song of Solomon. This marriage song may be very ancient, possibly even Canaanite in origin, but its presence in the canon attests to its acceptance by generations of Israelites. Two songs (chs. 1:2f. and 8:1–4) by the girl convey the intensity and beauty of her feeling for her beloved. The first opens with the words:

O that you would kiss me with the kisses of your mouth!
For your love is better than wine.

In spite of the recognition of the attraction between
the sexes, there are relatively few descriptions in the Old
Testament of the physical basis of that appeal. We have
already recorded one of them, the comment that Leah
had weak eyes but that Rachel was beautiful (Gen. 29:17).
Only in The Song of Solomon do we find a catalog of
feminine beauty. It is quite explicit. The sensuous passage in ch. 7:1–9 opens:

> How graceful are your feet in sandals,
>   O queenly maiden!
> Your rounded thighs are like jewels,
>   the work of a master hand.
>
> (Ch. 7:1)

It continues with an explicit description of the rest of the
girl's physical appeal (see also ch. 4:1–8). The description in ch. 6:4–7 is more restrained.

Elsewhere in the Old Testament the authors con-
tented themselves merely with noting that a woman was
beautiful. The strength of the bond of affection between
Absalom and the sister whom he avenged may be revealed in the notation, "There were born to Absalom
three sons, and one daughter whose name was Tamar;
she was a beautiful woman" (II Sam. 14:27), since Tamar
also was the name of Absalom's sister. The author of the
prose narrative of Job (Job 1:1 to 2:13; 42:7–17) empha-
sized the degree to which God repaid Job for his faithfulness under suffering by writing: "He had also seven sons
and three daughters. . . . And in all the land there were
no women so fair as Job's daughters" (ch. 42:13, 15).

One of the most unusual references to a woman's
beauty in the whole of the Old Testament appears in
Esth. 1:10–12. The king had been feasting and drinking
with his nobles for seven days, just as the queen had been

feasting and drinking with the wives for seven days. The king, self-restraint impaired, wanted the queen brought out of the harem in order to display her beauty; but the queen refused to be displayed!

There are approximately as many descriptions of male as of female beauty in the Old Testament. Some of them are given without mentioning feminine interest, as when it is said of the boy David that "he was ruddy, and had beautiful eyes, and was handsome" (I Sam. 16:12). In The Song of Solomon, however, where we find the most detailed descriptions of feminine beauty, we also find extended descriptions of the groom. "My beloved is all radiant and ruddy, distinguished among ten thousand" (S. of Sol. 5:10), sings the bride; and she proceeds to extol various parts of his body (vs. 11–16; see also chs. 2:8f.; 3:6–11).

IV

The timeless theme of the strength of the attraction of each sex for the other emerges not only in The Song of Solomon (where we would expect it) but also in the lament of David for the death of Saul and Jonathan and in post-exilic wisdom literature.

The passion of the bride for the groom is pictured in S. of Sol. 3:1–5 in a song that opens:

> Upon my bed at night
> I sought him whom my soul loves.
>> (See also ch. 5:2–8)

The groom's passion for the bride is stated all the more forcefully for being phrased so obliquely:

> Solomon had a vineyard at Baal-hammon;
> he let out the vineyard to keepers;

> each one was to bring for its fruit a thousand
>   pieces of silver.
> My vineyard, my very own, is for myself;
>   you, O Solomon, may have the thousand,
>   and the keepers of the fruit two hundred.
>   (S. of Sol. 8:11f.)

For the groom, the bride is worth more than the huge
rent paid the king for his vineyard.

The power of the love of a woman for a man, or of a
man for a woman, is expressed outside The Song of
Solomon in interesting ways. Several examples of it in its
most enduring form will be cited in the description of the
love that sustained married couples. Here, only three
other passages need be mentioned. In his lament over
the deaths of Saul and Jonathan, David described his
friendship with Jonathan as "wonderful, passing the love
of women" (II Sam. 1:26). Since we have abundant evidence of David's heterosexuality, this verse has to be
taken as the attempt to convey the intensity of a friendship by a comparison with the most widely shared form
of strong interpersonal ties.

The wisdom literature provides us with the well-
known series of comparisons:

> Three things are too wonderful for me;
>   four I do not understand:
> the way of an eagle in the sky,
>   the way of a serpent on a rock,
> the way of a ship on the high seas,
>   and the way of a man with a maiden.
>   (Prov. 30:18f.)

William McKane has written of these: "The key lies in the
recognition that the first three are parables of the mystery of man's desire for a woman or perhaps rather for
the irresistible and inexplicable attraction which draws
together the man and the woman."[17] Observation and

common sense tend to dominate the book of The Proverbs. Here, however, the sage comments on something he has observed but cannot reduce to common sense.

The strangest testimony in the Old Testament to the power of sexual attraction comes in the proclamation of Job's righteousness:

> I have made a covenant with my eyes;
>   how then could I look upon a virgin?
>   (Job 31:1)

This anticipates Jesus' teaching on adultery as reported in Matt. 5:27f.: "You have heard that it was said, 'You shall not commit adultery.' But I say to you that every one who looks at a woman lustfully has already committed adultery with her in his heart." In The Book of Job the issue is not so much adultery as conduct which protects Job from being attracted by the charms of any woman other than his wife.

V

Three conclusions stated earlier are confirmed by the evidence presented in this chapter.

The attraction of each sex for the other is normal, and The Song of Solomon celebrates this attraction explicitly and lyrically. The presence of this writing in the canon is often explained on the basis of the allegorical interpretation of the Lord as husband of Israel. In the light of materials gathered for this study of the status of woman in the Old Testament, however, it seems more likely that The Song of Solomon was included in the canon for a quite different reason. If usage by the community of faith was the decisive factor in canonization, we should seek a usage for The Song of Solomon appropriate both to its contents and to basic religious convictions of the community of faith. Evidence presented here demonstrates that sexuality, together with its consequences, and the family built upon it was seen in ancient Israel as a primary area for divine activity. Thus The Song of Solomon probably was used for its evident value, as a means for the joyful celebration of sexuality and marriage; and this corresponds to the attitude toward the creation of male and female stated in Gen. 1:27f.

The second conclusion is that the sexes are given virtual parity in the description of the explicitness and strength of sexual attraction.

The third conclusion is that woman is not condemned because of her attraction for man. The conduct of David and Amnon is condemned, but neither Bathsheba nor Tamar is criticized. A promiscuous woman is condemned in Prov. 5:20–23, yet this injunction against adultery opens with praise of sexual relations in marriage (vs. 15–19). This is in contrast to the tendency in later Judaism and Christianity to hold woman to be evil because of her attractiveness to man. That the Old Testament places limits on the expression of human sexuality, however, will be made clear later.

CHAPTER 3

Marriage

I

We tend to overlook the primacy of the family in the Old Testament. The divine promise given Abraham describes humanity as "all the families of the earth" (Gen. 12:3), and the transmission of that promise from Abraham down to the enslavement of Israel in Egypt is told as family history. Family genealogies appear throughout the Pentateuch, and there is more interest in the family affairs of the kings than in their statesmanship. In the late post-exilic rewriting of the history reported earlier in Samuel-Kings, the Chronicler provides elaborate and detailed family genealogies. Even in the book of The Proverbs, which may have been a series of exercises for the training of professional scribes, the sayings by means of which literacy and morality were taught dwell as often upon family relationships as upon those affairs of government and business which would be the duties of the future scribes.

The family was the primary structure of society throughout the whole period of time covered by the writings of the Old Testament. It was the source of biological

survival, it gave individuals their personal identity, it provided whatever economic security there was, and it was
the primary entity in legal and governmental affairs. To
describe a person's place in the family, therefore, is to
report the basis of his or her status in society.

Our study of the status of woman in the home will
occupy five chapters, those dealing with marriage, motherhood, the subservience of women, subservience to
women, and woman as sister, divorcée, and widow.

II

The continuation of the family through contracting
marriages for the children was the responsibility of the
family itself. This function is assigned to the father frequently in the Old Testament, although others also are
reported to have discharged the responsibility.

We are told several times that fathers "took wives" for
their sons. Judah "took a wife for Er his first-born," and
then tried to arrange a levirate marriage for his son's
widow in order to secure male issue for his dead son
(Gen. 38:6–9). The Chronicler reports that Rehoboam,
king of Judah, "procured wives" for all his sons (II
Chron. 11:23; see also ch. 18:1).

Fathers also are reported to give their daughters in
marriage. In the earliest of the narratives about Moses
(the J source), Reuel, a priest of Midian, gave his daughter Zipporah to Moses for Moses' wife (Ex. 2:21). Caleb
is said to have promised Achsah, his daughter, to anyone
who would capture Kiriath-sepher (Josh. 15:16 = Judg.
1:12). Samson's Philistine father-in-law, having decided
that Samson had repudiated his daughter, gave her in
marriage to one of Samson's friends (Judg. 15:2), and the
men of the Israelite confederation that had sworn during
a civil war not to give their daughters in marriage to the

men of the tribe of Benjamin relented and agreed to let
the Benjaminites capture wives for themselves during a
vintage festival (Judg. 21:1–23). Saul is reported twice to
have promised David one of his daughters (I Sam. 18:
17–19, 20–27). And Jeremiah is reported by Baruch, his
biographer, to have advised the Judeans taken into exile
in Babylonia in 598 b.c. to "take wives and have sons and
daughters; take wives for your sons, and give your daughters in marriage" (Jer. 29:6).

Others could act on behalf of the family. Rebekah's
brother and mother represented her family in some of
the marriage negotiations with Abraham's representative
seeking a bride for Isaac (Gen. 24:28–51) even though
Bethuel, her father, was present (vs. 15, 50); and
Jehoiada, a priest, secured wives for the young king for
whom he was acting as regent (II Chron. 24:2f.).

The passages just cited could be taken as proof that
the ancient Israelite father when living so dominated the
family that he alone contracted marriages for his children. Other passages, however, indicate that the matter
was not quite that simple. Samson's marriage to a Philistine girl was arranged by his parents under protest because Samson insisted upon it (Judg. 14:1–4). Similarly,
in the legendary story of a clash between the city of
Shechem and invading Israelites, Shechem, pictured as a
youth, raped an Israelite girl and then asked his father to
arrange a marriage (Gen. 34:1–4). Father and son sought
to negotiate it together (vs. 5–12), and the girl was represented by both father and brothers (vs. 7, 13–17).

Other passages report the groom acting on his own
behalf. The patriarch Judah is said to have taken a Canaanite girl as wife (Gen. 38:2), and the legal restrictions
placed on a priest's marriage say nothing about the participation of the parents in his choice (Lev. 21:13–15;
Ezek. 44:22). Leviticus, ch. 21, is post-exilic. The pre-
exilic Deuteronomic Code provided for marriage to a

woman captured in war, again without any reference to the husband's parents (Deut. 21:10–14).

A prophet might marry as a "sign," a deed that was to convey a word from the Lord. This is reported of Hosea twice, in both instances obscurely. "When the LORD first spoke through Hosea, the LORD said to Hosea, 'Go, take to yourself a wife of harlotry and have children of harlotry, for the land commits great harlotry by forsaking the LORD'" (Hos. 1:2). The meaning of the phrase "a wife of harlotry" is unclear. Following Hosea's divorce, he again received a word from the Lord: "And the LORD said to me, 'Go again, love a woman who is beloved of a paramour and is an adulteress; even as the LORD loves the people of Israel, though they turn to other gods and love cakes of raisins'" (Hos. 3:1). Here it is not clear whether the prophet is attracted for the second time to his first wife (as I believe) or to a second woman. In neither of these passages is the prophet's father mentioned. Nor is Hilkiah, Jeremiah's father, when that prophet heard "the word of the LORD," "You shall not take a wife, nor shall you have sons or daughters in this place" (Jer. 16:2). Hosea's marriage was to be an acting out of the relationship between the Lord and Israel, in which Gomer's infidelity to Hosea paralleled Israel's faithlessness to God. Jeremiah was commanded not to marry as a sign of the divine judgment against Judah.

The king seems often to have arranged marriages for himself. One of the narrative strands telling of David's rise to the throne pictures him as the captain of a band of mercenaries. An incident in this strand involves Nabal, a wealthy man who refuses to buy protection from David. Nabal's wife Abigail, however, provided the tribute. Her deed so enraged Nabal that he dropped dead when she told him about it. "Then David sent and wooed Abigail, to make her his wife" (I Sam. 25:39).

Princes are reported twice as seeking to take wives for

themselves in the attempt to establish a claim on the throne by possessing the former king's harem. Absalom did this during his revolt against David (II Sam. 16: 20–22), and Adonijah, the older son displaced by Solomon's seizure of the throne, tried to strengthen his claim to be king by attempting to marry Abishag, David's last concubine. Solomon replied to the person transmitting the request: "And why do you ask Abishag the Shunammite for Adonijah? Ask for him the kingdom also; for he is my elder brother, and on his side are Abiathar the priest and Joab the son of Zeruiah" (I Kings 2:22).[18]

Marriages arranged by kings seem often to have represented alliances between royal houses. Solomon made "a marriage alliance with Pharaoh king of Egypt" (I Kings 3:1) which probably reflected Egyptian foreign policy and gave Solomon status. The seven hundred princesses that he married (ch. 11:3) may have represented as many alliances.

A final situation in which a man chose his own wife can be reported best in the words of the Deuteronomic law code:

> If a man meets a virgin who is not betrothed, and seizes her and lies with her, and they are found, then the man who lay with her shall give to the father of the young woman fifty shekels of silver, and she shall be his wife, because he has violated her; he may not put her away all his days. (Deut. 22:28f.)

This is a form of marriage by capture in which the captor is captured!

A woman also could display initiative in arranging marriage. Instances of this in the Old Testament are rare, yet the practice seems to have been sufficiently acceptable to be reported without comment. We have already noted that Michal's love for David was well known in Saul's court before there had been any thought of giving

her to David as wife (I Sam. 18:20). Tamar, David's
daughter, tried to change the threat of rape by Amnon
into marriage, replying to his demand that she lie with
him:

> No, my brother, do not force me; for such a thing is not done
> in Israel; do not do this wanton folly. And as for me, where
> could I carry my shame? And as for you, you would be as one
> of the wanton fools in Israel. Now therefore, I pray you,
> speak to the king; for he will not withhold me from you. (II
> Sam. 13:12–13)

Daughters whose father had died without male issue
inherited the family property and chose their own husbands, according to decisions made about the daughters
of Zelophehad (Num. 27:1–11; 36:1–12). There was one
condition: "Let them marry whom they think best; only,
they shall marry within the family of the tribe of their
father" (Num. 36:6b).

Two other incidents indicate that the bride shared in
the decisions involved in the marriage. When the servant
who represented Abraham, the father of the groom
(Isaac), urged Rebekah's family to allow her to leave with
him immediately, they said, " 'We will call the maiden,
and ask her.' And they called Rebekah, and said to her,
'Will you go with this man?' She said, 'I will go' " (Gen.
24:57f.). Abigail displayed a similar decisiveness when
David asked her to become his wife (I Sam. 25:40–42).
Rebekah was a dependent virgin, and Abigail was a
widow; but each decided when to join her future husband
and thus determined when the marriage would be con-
summated. Abigail also seems to have decided to accept
David's proposal. No male relative is mentioned.

The passages we have just examined suggest that the
contracting of a marriage was a family matter. The person (or persons) who was the functioning head of the
family seems to have had the formal responsibility for

arranging marriage for both sons and daughters. This individual often was the father, although husbands and wives are described as acting together. The person to be married, whether female or male, could have the responsibility if he or she were the *de facto* head of the family. There also is evidence that the wishes of the bride and groom were influential.

III

What kind of transaction was marriage? Was the daughter sold? Was an unmarried female disposable property? These questions must be asked because passages in the Old Testament seem to imply the purchase of the bride. Bride purchase appears to be reported in Ex. 22:16f.:

> If a man seduces a virgin who is not betrothed, and lies with her, he shall give the marriage present for her, and make her his wife. If her father utterly refuses to give her to him, he shall pay money equivalent to the marriage present for virgins.

Shechem, in Gen. 34:12, promises to provide whatever "marriage present and gift" is asked.[19] The matter cannot be left here, however. This is a scanty sampling of the reports in the Old Testament of exchanges of property accompanying marriage.

There is at least one reference in the Old Testament to gifts given the bride by the father of the groom. In the story of the betrothal of Rebekah and Isaac, we are told that the servant representing Abraham "brought forth jewelry of silver and of gold, and raiment, and gave them to Rebekah" (Gen. 24:53).

The "marriage money" for virgins mentioned in Ex. 22:16f. presumably was paid to the family of the bride, but other narratives describe a father asking of a prospective groom seven years' service (Gen. 29:16–30; Hos. 12:12), circumcision (Gen. 34:12–17), the capture of a city (Josh. 15:16 = Judg. 1:12), and military service (I Sam. 18:17–27). Each of these was of substantial value to the family of the bride.

The bride often seems to have received a gift from her own family. When Laban "gave" Leah and Rachel to Jacob, he gave each girl a servant (Gen. 29:24, 29). Caleb's daughter, after being given in marriage to Othniel, then asked her father to give her springs of water (Josh. 15:19 = Judg. 1:15). And we are told that Pharaoh, king of Egypt, gave Gezer as a dowry to his daughter, Solomon's wife (I Kings 9:16).

There is an odd sequel to the service Jacob gave his father-in-law for Leah and Rachel. When Jacob described to his wives how their father had cheated him, "then Rachel and Leah answered him, 'Is there any portion or inheritance left to us in our father's house? Are we not regarded by him as foreigners? For he has sold us, and he has been using up the money given for us'" (Gen. 31:14f.). Apparently the daughters felt themselves to have been wronged by their father, to have been treated as if they were "foreigners," not as daughters.

How is all of this evidence to be interpreted? The Covenant Code, a Canaanite law code adapted by the Israelites to their own use, provides for the sale of a daughter:

> When a man sells his daughter as a slave, she shall not go out as the male slaves do. If she does not please her master, who has designated her for himself, then he shall let her be redeemed; he shall have no right to sell her to a foreign people, since he has dealt faithlessly with her. If he designates her for his son, he shall deal with her as with a daughter. If he takes another wife to himself, he shall not diminish her food, her clothing, or her marital rights. And if he does

not do these three things for her, she shall go out for nothing, without payment of money. (Ex. 21:7–11)

Both sons and daughters could be sold into slavery by their parents. This law restricts the type of servitude to which the daughter could be subjected and protects her rights while she was enslaved. The slavery here is a form of marriage. This and the bitter comment by Leah and Rachel in Gen. 31:14f. constitute the primary evidence in support for the hypothesis that a daughter was negotiable property.

The variety of donors and recipients of marriage gifts makes it difficult to maintain that the bride had been sold by her family. The evidence available to us suggests strongly that selfhood for the ancient Israelite was corporate rather than individualistic, and that the fundamental reality in it was the family group in its totality.[20] Since that totality included every person in the family, as well as all that the family owned, the movement of children from one family to another through marriage would seem to change the relative strength of the families involved. It is possible that the exchange of wedding gifts was a redress of the original relative strengths of the families of bride and groom.

The evidence we have surveyed, however, does not seem to support such an interpretation. It was not always the family of the groom which gave a present to the family of the bride, yet the groom's family had been enlarged by the addition to it of the bride. Millar Burrows suggested, "The gift established a bond not merely by creating good will or a sense of obligation but by actually conveying something of the life of the giver to the recipient."[21] This implies that marriage represented a fusion of the families involved. The exchange of gifts would thus become a part of that merger.

The suggestion that marriage was a merger of the

families involved is supported by two passages. Shechem
and his father urge their fellow townsmen to pay the
"price" asked for Dinah, saying:

> Only on this condition will the men agree to dwell with us,
> to become one people: that every male among us be circum-
> cised as they are circumcised. Will not their cattle, their
> property, and all their beasts be ours? Only let us agree with
> them, and they will dwell with us. (Gen. 34:22f.)

Nehemiah, seeking to rebuild Jerusalem after the exile of
586 to 536 B.C., found himself hindered by a Samaritan
named Tobiah. He was powerful, since "many in Judah
were bound by oath to him, because he was the son-in-
law of Shecaniah the son of Arah: and his son Jehohanan
had taken the daughter of Meshullam the son of Bere-
chiah as his wife" (Neh. 6:18). Family ties created by
marriage were stronger than regional loyalties.

Thus the giving of gifts during a marriage does not
imply a subordinate status for the bride, whether we view
the exchange as a redress of the relative strength of the
two families or as a celebration of the fusion of the two
families. Quite the contrary! Even the law governing the
sale of a daughter into slavery indicates her high standing. She could be sold only for a form of marriage; she
could not be resold; and her marital rights could not be
reduced. No such protection was given a son sold into
slavery.

IV

The practice of polygamy in ancient Israel has been
held on three counts to imply an inferior status for the
wife. The purpose of marriage has been said to be to
perpetuate the husband's name, and "two or three wives
do more than one to satisfy the husband's demand for

progeny."[22] The ability of the husband to support a harem was a form of conspicuous consumption, a witness to the standing of the man in the community.[23] And the existence of the institution gave rise to a double standard which discriminated against the wife. It is sometimes claimed that only the wife could commit adultery in a polygamous marriage. The man involved had merely violated another man's property rights. Once again, however, we need to measure our expectation of what we will find in the Old Testament by what the Old Testament itself reports.

Polygamy was practiced in ancient Israel. Jacob had two wives and two concubines (Gen., chs. 29 to 30). Gideon had many wives and a concubine (Judg. 8:30f.); Elkanah had two wives (I Sam. 1:2); David had a harem of unspecified size (I Chron. 14:3); Solomon had seven hundred wives and three hundred concubines (I Kings 11:3); Rehoboam had eighteen wives and sixty concubines (II Chron. 11:21); and Abijah married fourteen wives (II Chron. 13:21). David, Solomon, Rehoboam, and Abijah were kings.

There also are references in the Old Testament to the kinds of family relationships possible only in a polygamous marriage. Gideon described slain men as "my brothers, the sons of my mother" (Judg. 8:19), indicating a distinction between them and other brothers with whom only the father was shared. Abimelech claimed a relationship with his mother's relatives and their city that brothers who had different mothers lacked (Judg. 9:1–3). Jephthah's paternal brothers excluded him from their patrimony because his mother had been a harlot (Judg. 11:2). Amnon and Absalom were half brothers, sons of different mothers (Ahinoam for Amnon and Maacah for Absalom, II Sam. 3:2f.). The Deuteronomic law code also attests to the practice of polygamy by stipulating that a man, in settling his estate, "may not treat the son of the loved as the first-born in preference to the son of the disliked, who is the first-born" (Deut. 21:16; see also Ex. 21:10; Lev. 18:18).

It is often said that monogamy was more common than polygamy in ancient Israel.[24] Both the direct and the indirect evidence seem to bear this out. Samson's father had one wife (Judg. 13:2; 14:2–4), as did Uriah, Bath-sheba's first husband (II Sam. 11:3; 12:1–7), Ezekiel (Ezek. 24:15–18), and Job (Job 2:9f.). It also seems proper to infer monogamy from such comments in The Proverbs as

> It is better to live in a corner of the housetop
> than in a house shared with a contentious woman
> (Prov. 21:9; 25:24)

or from the advice given a youth in Prov. 5:18f. In fact, instances of polygamy reported outside royal families are confined to the pre-monarchic period, although we should perhaps not make too much of this.

Indirect evidence of opposition to polygamy is found in the Deuteronomists' suspicion, stated both in the law code and in the history, that it encouraged apostasy. Deuteronomy 17:17 warns, "And he [the king] shall not multiply wives for himself, lest his heart turn away; nor shall he greatly multiply for himself silver and gold." A similar attitude reappears in the Deuteronomic historian's comment about Solomon's harem (I Kings 11: 4–8).

We cannot have it both ways in attempting to assess the significance of the practice of polygamy in ancient Israel for the status of woman. If we believe that polygamy lowered the status of woman, then monogamy raised it. It seems likely to me, however, that neither form of marriage contributes to our knowledge of the standing of woman. We will see later that even the law codes which acknowledge polygamy are as harsh in their treatment of the man involved in adultery as of the woman. Thus polygamy did not encourage a double standard. The influence of the members of the harem on the religion of the husband was such as to give rise to the suspicion that the wives exercised a good deal of power individually and collectively. It may be better to view polygamy as an attempt to ensure the survival of the family in the face of what must have been a shocking mortality rate among mothers and infants rather than as an expression of male supremacy.

V

Two other aspects of Old Testament evidence dealing with marriage yield information important for understanding the status of woman. These are the value put upon marriage, and reports of marital love.

Several oracles of judgment and restoration employ similes taken from marriage. A psalmist conveyed the devastation of the experience of divine judgment by writing:

> Fire devoured their young men,
>   and their maidens had no marriage song.
> (Ps. 78:63)

This image is found also in Jer. 7:34. Jeremiah used the contrast between a bride's care for her finery and the nation's neglect of its God to give force to a proclamation of judgment (Jer. 2:32). Elsewhere he described a nation faithful to God as a bride that "followed me [God] in the wilderness, in a land not sown" (ch. 2:2).

The focus of passages of this kind is upon the relationship between God and people. The effectiveness of the simile depends upon its importance in the minds of those who use or hear it. Thus the use of the marriage bond

and festivities in statements about the relationship between God and people is strong evidence of the high
standing given marriage. Since only the bride is mentioned several times (e.g., Jer. 2:2f., 32; Ps. 78:63; Joel
1:8), it seems proper to conclude that her status must
have been high for her role to have sustained the importance given it in the similes.

Reports in the Old Testament of marital love gain
added luster when they are read against the background
of the candid descriptions of marital discord also found
in the Scriptures. Proverbs 27:15f., because of its wry
humor, can represent all other passages of like view-
point:

> A continual dripping on a rainy day
>   and a contentious woman are alike;
> to restrain her is to restrain the wind
>   or to grasp oil in his right hand.

By contrast, the tributes to the depth and duration of
marital love that appear in the Old Testament are all
the more impressive because they are so oblique. It is
almost as if feelings ran so deeply that they were hard
to voice.

Each year, Elkanah and his two wives went together to
a festival at Shiloh. When Peninnah, who had children,
taunted Hannah, who was childless, Elkanah tried to con-
sole Hannah, saying: "Why do you weep? And why do
you not eat? And why is your heart sad? Am I not more
to you than ten sons?" (I Sam. 1:8). Children were so
important in an Israelite marriage that Elkanah knew why
Hannah was sad and shared her sadness. Therefore his
words come to us across the centuries as those of a husband trying to make the best of a situation in which two
people who loved one another found themselves.

One tribute to married love appears in a law on the
freeing of slaves:

If his master gives him [a Hebrew slave] a wife and she bears him sons or daughters, the wife and her children shall be her master's and he shall go out alone. But if the slave plainly says, "I love my master, my wife, and my children; I will not go out free," then his master shall bring him to God, and he shall bring him to the door or the doorpost; and his master shall bore his ear through with an awl; and he shall serve him for life. (Ex. 21:4–6)

The Israelites' love of their rights and their freedom is writ large in the pages of the Old Testament. That there were enough who loved their slave wives more than their freedom to make this law necessary is quite a tribute to the love that sustained those marriages.

Our deepest feelings are likely to emerge most clearly in the elemental crises of life. It is not surprising that testimony to the love of man and wife should appear in the report of the death of the one or the other. One example is the report of Sarah's death (Gen. 23:1f.). Another is Ezekiel's description of the death of his wife:

Also the word of the LORD came to me: "Son of man, behold, I am about to take the delight of your eyes away from you at a stroke; yet you shall not mourn or weep nor shall your tears run down. Sigh, but not aloud; make no mourning for the dead. Bind on your turban, and put your shoes on your feet; do not cover your lips, nor eat the bread of mourners." So I spoke to the people in the morning, and at evening my wife died. And on the next morning I did as I was commanded. (Ezek. 24:15–18)

Ezekiel had been commanded to announce a terrible event in which the victims would not be allowed to mourn for their dead, the devastation of Judah and the capture of Jerusalem. He was to proclaim the word of the Lord by not mourning after the death of his beloved wife. For the acted sign to have been recognized as such, the group of exiles to which it was directed must have had prior knowledge of the couple's love for one another.

Because we opened this section with one of the tart comments of the sages about wives, we should add here the sardonic observation of the author of Ecclesiastes on the meaninglessness of life:

> Enjoy life with the wife whom you love, all the days of your vain life which he has given you under the sun, because that is your portion in life and in your toil at which you toil under the sun. Whatever your hand finds to do, do it with your might; for there is no work or thought or knowledge or wisdom in Sheol, to which you are going. (Eccl. 9:9f.)

But at least do whatever you do with the wife whom you love! Roland de Vaux wrote: "Those rare passages which give us a glimpse into the intimacy of family life show that an Israelite wife was loved and listened to by her husband, and treated by him as an equal. . . . And there is no doubt that this was the normal picture."[25] Evidence has been submitted here which indicates that it was a part of the normal picture, but only a part, for we read of alienation and hostility also.

Exodus 20:17 is often quoted in support of the contention that the wife in ancient Israel was the property of her husband: "You shall not covet your neighbor's house; you shall not covet your neighbor's wife, or his manservant, or his maidservant, or his ox, or his ass, or anything that is your neighbor's." The evidence we have just reviewed, however, is the most convincing demonstration that such a view of woman in ancient Israel cannot be correct. The strength and durability of the bond between husband and wife (and also the depth of alienation and hostility) which we have just seen could exist only between persons who lived together within a framework of mutual respect. The love that sustained Abraham and Sarah until she was 127 years old was no momentary physical attraction, and the agony of a prophet acting out the destruction of his nation in his conduct after the death of his wife is not the affection of a man for a prized possession.

What we have just glimpsed is an understanding of the bond between man and wife in marriage which continues to this day to be the most demanding concept of marriage known to us. The author of Gen. 2:24 stated it when he wrote, "Therefore a man leaves his father and his mother and cleaves to his wife, and they become one flesh." The two become one! Again, as in the P creation story (Gen. 1:26f.), the status of the husband is the status of the wife, and the status of the wife is the status of the husband.

VI

This has been a long and tortuous road. Nonetheless, important conclusions have been reached along the way. We have encountered the first evidence of a parity between the sexes in which there is some functional differentiation. Fathers are said often to have arranged the marriages of children, yet other passages giving us more details tell us that virtually all concerned participated— mothers, brides, grooms, and brothers. No examples have survived of a father assigning a daughter to a marriage against her will. From this, it was concluded that arranging marriages was a family concern in which the bride and groom had a significant role. The father seems to have acted as the representative of the group, its epitome. Except in royal marriages, where different expectations may have prevailed, wives, daughters, and sons had too decisive a part to play to use any language that implies tyrannical powers for the father.

The familial significance of marriage was confirmed further by the exchange of gifts before and after the event. Interpretations of this practice which see it as the sale of the bride by her father and the purchase of the girl by the father of the groom simply ignore the passages indicating a widespread distribution of gifts throughout both families. No bride-purchase hypothesis fits all the facts. Instead, we found it necessary to turn to a different hypothesis. The daughter and son were so valued by their respective families that changes in their standing in their own families called for either a carefully balanced system of mutual compensation for loss or an equally carefully calculated manifestation of the fusion of the two families. The practice among royal families and the families of the nobility of making alliances through marriage support the second possibility rather than the first. In either case, the inadvertent testimony of the material underscores the high status of the bride, both in her own family and in the groom's.

No particular significance for the status of woman was found in the practice of both polygamy and monogamy. The use of the bride as a simile for Israel in its relationships with God under the covenant, and the infrequent but moving testimonies to marital love, were found to be indirect but strong evidence of the extremely high status of woman in ancient Israel.

This chapter, because of the nature of its subject matter, found more evidence for the high standing of the woman than of the man, but it also reported one area in which the husband often (but not always) occupied an office on behalf of the family. In the next chapter, we will examine the unique function of woman in the Old Testament. Later chapters will demonstrate, however, that her unique function was far from her only function.

CHAPTER 4

Woman as Mother

I

We need to keep in mind the precariousness of survival in ancient Palestine as we begin our study of the status of the Israelite mother. On the basis of medical records from our own not too distant past, we have to assume an extremely high rate of infant and maternal mortality. II Chronicles 11:21 and 13:21 may preserve a hint of this. Rehoboam's 78 consorts (18 wives and 60 concubines) bore only eighty-eight children for an average of only one and thirteen hundredth's children each. Abijah's 14 wives had thirty-eight children for.an average of two and one tenth each. Presumably these totals list only surviving children. A very high mortality rate in the population as a whole from infection, disease, famine, and war must be added to the high infant and maternal mortality rate.

Group survival must have been the primary issue facing the Israelites most of the time. The childbearers, those who replenished the strength of the family, may be presumed to have had an importance in ancient Israel nearly inconceivable to those of us living in an age facing overpopulation. Preoccupation with survival, therefore, is the context out of which one important part of the record of the status of woman in the Old Testament was written.

The role of woman as mother will be studied under three major headings: childbearing and bereavement, conception and birth, and the care of children.

II

Childbearing was a social function in ancient Israel, and fecundity, barrenness, and the loss of children were of urgent concern to men, women, and the nation.

Two late passages and a description of the Levirate illustrate the importance of offspring for the husband. The first passage is a wisdom psalm which describes the blessing given the righteous man:

> Your wife will be like a fruitful vine
> within your house;
> your children will be like olive shoots
> around your table.
> Lo, thus shall the man be blessed
> who fears the LORD.
>
> (Ps. 128:3f.)

The second example, Is. 56:4f., is one of the group of late poems with which The Book of Isaiah closes. Here, eunuchs who are faithful to the Lord are promised "a monument and a name better than sons and daughters." Daughters and sons must have been very important for them to have been the norm by which divine reward was measured!

The Levirate conveys to us the importance of a wife who bore sons for her husband. The legal provision for the practice describes it clearly:

> If brothers dwell together, and one of them dies and has no
> son, the wife of the dead shall not be married outside the
> family to a stranger; her husband's brother shall go in to her,
> and take her as his wife, and perform the duty of a husband's
> brother to her. And the first son whom she bears shall suc-
> ceed to the name of his brother who is dead, that his name
> may not be blotted out of Israel. (Deut. 25:5f.)

The latter half of the law (vs. 7–10) deals with the punishment of the man who refuses to perform the duty. The
widow could protest to the village elders. Should he continue to evade his responsibility, the widow could insult
him and his family.

The law of the Levirate is the basis of two narratives,
the story of the patriarch Judah and his daughter-in-law
Tamar (Gen. 38:6–26) and The Book of Ruth. Practices
in The Book of Ruth deviate from the Levirate as described in Deut. 25:5–10. The book contains other enig-
mas also. But the narrative in Gen., ch. 38, is based upon
the law as we have just seen it defined in Deuteronomy:

> And Judah took a wife for Er his first-born, and her name was
> Tamar. But Er, Judah's first-born, was wicked in the sight of
> the LORD, and the LORD slew him. Then Judah said to Onan,
> "Go in to your brother's wife, and perform the duty of a
> brother-in-law to her, and raise up offspring for your
> brother." But Onan knew that the offspring would not be
> his; so when he went in to his brother's wife he spilled the
> semen on the ground, lest he should give offspring to his
> brother. And what he did was displeasing in the sight of the
> LORD, and he slew him also. Then Judah said to Tamar his
> daughter-in-law, "Remain a widow in your father's house,
> till Shelah my son grows up." (Gen. 38:6–11a)

But Shelah was not given to Tamar as her husband.

When Judah went out to supervise some sheep-shear-
ing, Tamar disguised herself as a prostitute and waited
beside the road. Judah saw her, did not recognize her,
and patronized her. He left his signet and staff in pledge

for a kid from the flock to be delivered later as payment. After he left, Tamar removed her disguise and returned home. Judah's servants, trying to deliver the kid, could find no one and could not redeem Judah's signet and staff.

When Tamar later was found to be pregnant, Judah commanded that she be killed. He revoked his order when she proved his paternity by producing his signet and staff (vs. 24f.) She was guilty of adultery to her dead husband, but Judah was guilty of not making available to her another of his sons. He himself judged his offense to have been the greater (v. 26). The conclusion of the story, incidentally, is that she bore twins, both sons.

Other passages also make clear the importance of sons to the husband. Leah, the wife with the weak eyes, was fecund, and Rachel, whom Jacob loved, was barren. According to popular tradition, the names that Leah gave her sons reflected her hope that Jacob would come to love her because of the sons she was bearing him:

> And Leah conceived and bore a son, and she called his name Reuben [i.e., "See, a son"]; for she said, "Because the Lord has looked upon my affliction; surely now my husband will love me." (Gen. 29:32; see vs. 33f. for the births of Simeon and Levi)

Other passages report women's attitude toward the mother of sons. Rachel, in fatal labor, was encouraged by the midwife, "Fear not; for now you will have another son" (Gen. 35:17), as was the wife of Phinehas in like circumstances (I Sam. 4:20). And Naomi's grandson is described as "a restorer of life and a nourisher of your old age" (Ruth 4:15) by the women of the village. Even pregnancy without hint of the sex of the child was greatly desired. When Sarai saw that she was barren, she gave Abram her maidservant, Hagar, as a concubine. When

Hagar conceived, she looked with contempt on her mistress (Gen. 16:4).

The intensity of women's longing for sons is epitomized by Rachel's cry to Jacob, "Give me children, or I shall die!" (Gen. 30:1b). For the time being, Rachel had to be content with seeking sons born to Jacob through the maidservant she had given him as a concubine.[26] Finally, "God remembered Rachel, and God hearkened to her and opened her womb. She conceived and bore a son, and said, 'God has taken away my reproach'; and she called his name Joseph [i.e., 'He adds'], saying, 'May the LORD add to me another son!' " (Gen. 30:22f.).

If further confirmation of the importance of sons be needed, it is provided by passages describing the severity of their loss. When Samuel killed Agag, the king of the Amalekites, he said, "As your sword has made women childless, so shall your mother be childless among women" (I Sam. 15:33). The wise woman of Tekoa, used by Joab to persuade David to restore Absalom to the court after Absalom had caused the death of a brother, represented herself as a widow who once had had two sons. One had killed the other, and the village elders wished to execute the survivor for his crime. "Thus they would quench my coal which is left, and leave to my husband neither name nor remnant upon the face of the earth" (II Sam. 14:7b). This passage is particularly important because it identifies the concern of the mother both for herself and for her husband. Her spark of life would be extinguished, and her husband's family would be cut off.

We will return to the mother's concern for her "coal" in a different context. Here, we can complete our description of the genealogical importance of sons. The name "Isaac," given to the son of Abraham and Sarah, was derived from the root "laugh," and the Israelite's love for puns probably accounts for the evocation of the pun twice on the mother's lips and once on the father's (Gen. 12:12; 17:17–19; 21:6f.). Pun or not, however, the survival of Abraham's family was no laughing matter.

Abraham had been promised descendants by God (Gen. 12:2, 7; 13:16; etc.).[27] Each time the transmission of the promise seems threatened by events, divine activity is reported. During the Egyptian enslavement, when the Pharaoh commanded all male Israelite children to be killed (an edict which would have exterminated the descendants of Abraham in a single generation had it been enforced), the midwives who deceived the Egyptians are blessed by God and the people increased (Ex. 1:15–22). During the Babylonian exile, when the people were dispersed and their institutions had been disrupted, the Second Isaiah (the author of Isa., chs. 40 to 55) recalled the gift of a son to Abraham and Sarah:

> Look to Abraham your father
> and to Sarah who bore you;
> for when he was but one I called him,
> and I blessed him and made him many.
> (Isa. 51:2)

So certain was the prophet that God would honor his promise that Israel would be a mighty nation that he proclaimed as the word of the Lord to an enslaved and discouraged people:

> The children born in the time of your bereavement
> will yet say in your ears:
> "The place is too narrow for me;
> make room for me to dwell in."
> (Isa. 49:20)

As has been true here several times, we find confirmation in legislation of a motif stated in song and story. The Deuteronomic law code revived the ancient concept of the holy war, yet it held the siring of children to be so important that a member of the sacred militia was excused from military duty until he had had opportunity to beget offspring (Deut. 24:5).

The importance accorded the wife as mother is stated tersely by the Yahwist: "The man called his wife's name Eve, because she was the mother of all living" (Gen. 3:20). Every culture provides for specialization by function. In the Old Testament, the name of the husband provided continuity from generation to generation, and thus wives bore sons for their husbands. But the woman was given the awesome role of being "the mother of all living."

III

The description of a differentiation of function in the family is not enough by itself to permit us to derive a statement of the status, or the importance, of woman in the Old Testament. A further category of evidence is needed, a description of the ancient Israelite's knowledge of the process of conception and birth.

The Israelites understood something of the function of the male's semen in conception. This has already been reported in this chapter in the story of Judah's attempt to secure a son for a dead son by Onan, the deceased's brother. "But Onan knew that the offspring would not be his; so when he went in to his brother's wife he spilled the semen on the ground, lest he should give offspring to his brother" (Gen. 38:9). We also have the notation that Bathsheba conceived after David "lay with her" (II Sam. 11:4f.), and the report of Isaiah: "I went to the prophetess, and she conceived and bore a son" (Isa. 8:3a). What seems not to have been understood was the growth of the fetus in the womb. The author of Ecclesiastes, a late wisdom writing, used that mystery as a simile to describe the mystery of God's creative work elsewhere: "As you do not know the way of the wind, or how the bones grow in the womb of a woman with child, so you do not know the work of God who makes everything" (Eccl. 11:5).[28] Nor did they know why some women remained barren after cohabitation.

In place of our descriptions of biological processes, the ancient Israelite attributed conception (or barrenness) and the growth of the fetus to divine action. Samson's mother was barren until "the angel of the LORD appeared to the woman and said to her, 'Behold you are barren and have no children; but you shall conceive and bear a son' " (Judg. 13:3). The author of Ps. 113:9 wrote:

> He gives the barren woman a home,
>   making her the joyous mother of children.
> Praise the LORD!

When Rebekah, Isaac's wife, was barren, he "prayed to the LORD for his wife, because she was barren; and the LORD granted his prayer, and Rebekah his wife conceived" (Gen. 25:21).[29]

This theme is found in two of the great law codes. The Deuteronomic law code assured its readers that "there shall not be male or female barren among you, or among your cattle" (Deut. 7:14b; see also vs. 12f., 30:9f.) if they were faithful to their covenant with God. In the Priestly legislation, it is said of a woman acquitted in a trial resulting from a false charge of infidelity that "she shall be free and shall conceive children" (Num. 5:28).

Although God is sometimes said to have been responsible for opening the womb when the child being born was to become a "man of God," this is not as frequent as we would expect. We have already noted here that Samson's mother was told she would "conceive and bear a son" (Judg. 13:3) whom she is to rear as a Nazirite. Samuel was born when the Lord made Hannah fecund after her urgent prayers and her vow to dedicate the son to God's service (I Sam. 1:11). When she kept her vow, "the LORD visited Hannah, and she conceived and bore three sons and two daughters" (ch. 2:21a; see also Jer. 1:4f.). In the majority of cases, however, unusual divine participation is not claimed in the birth of a person later distinguished as a religious leader. No special intervention is recorded in the conception and birth of Moses, for example, or of any prophet other than Jeremiah.

There was an awareness of normal expectation in a woman's capacity to bear children. Sarah's amusement, when she heard that she was to bear a son, was because "it had ceased to be with Sarah after the manner of women" and because both she and her husband were old (Gen. 18:11f.). Elisha was befriended by a wealthy woman of Shunem who provided lodging and food when he was there. In return, he promised her a son. She replied, "No, my lord, O man of God; do not lie to your maidservant" (II Kings 4:16). In both of these cases, we are told that one or both of the parents was too old to expect to have children, apparently to underscore the magnitude of the intervention of God.

Since the Lord was believed to open the womb, God also was held to close it. We are told that God had made Rachel (Gen. 30:2) and Hannah (I Sam. 1:6) barren. In neither case was the husband or the wife said to have displeased God. In other passages, however, childlessness was attributed to sin. If a man lies with his uncle's wife, it will be counted a sin and "they shall die childless" (Lev. 20:20), as shall the woman if a man has intercourse with his brother's wife (v. 21). The bitter exchange between Michal and David after David had danced before the Ark of the Lord closes with the notation that Michal was childless to her death (II Sam. 6:20–23). The implication is that she was being punished for sin, although we are not told what the sin was. What was believed to be true of the individual was also held to be true of the nation, as in Hosea's tragic prophecy:

> Ephraim's glory shall fly away like a bird—
> no birth, no pregnancy, no conception!
>
> (Hos. 9:11)

God's involvement in conception and birth was so important to the ancient Israelites that they gave it extensive theological significance. When Onan evaded his duty toward his brother's widow, what he did "was displeasing in the sight of the LORD, and he slew him [Onan] also" (Gen. 38:9f.). In one of the curses with which The Book of Amos opens, the prophet speaks the word of the Lord against the Ammonites

> because they have ripped up women with child in Gilead,
> that they might enlarge their border.
>
> (Amos 1:13b)

In each of these passages, acts that disrupted the deed being done by the Lord in bringing children to birth are judged to be a sin of such gravity that the loss of the life of those guilty was required.

Because no child was born without the participation of the Lord, the birth of a child was a demonstration of God's active presence. Therefore a birth could become a "sign," or an acted word. This may have been the reason that Hosea and Isaiah gave their children names which contained a part of the word of the Lord given to the fathers to proclaim (Hos. 1:2–9; Isa. 7:3; 8:3f.). When the father's message changed, the child's name also apparently could change. Hosea's son "Not my people" became "My people," and the daughter "Not pitied" became "She has obtained pity" (Hos. 1:6, 9; 2:1). Such a name could be quite long. Isaiah's son Maher-shalal-hash-baz must have had a nickname!

This is the context in which one of the more controversial passages in the Old Testament prophets is to be understood:

> Therefore the Lord himself will give you a sign. Behold, a young woman shall conceive and bear a son, and shall call his name Immanuel. He shall eat curds and honey when he knows how to refuse the evil and choose the good. For before the child knows how to refuse the evil and choose the good, the land before whose two kings you are in dread will be deserted. (Isa. 7:14–16)

The same God who controlled the history of Judah also gave new life. The "sign," or proof that the word of the Lord spoken by Isaiah was true, was that the enemy feared by the king would be shattered before a child soon to be conceived could distinguish between good and evil. Giving children names which contained the deity's name or an allusion to the deity was done often in ancient Israel, as it is here. Immanuel means "God with us."

The word of the Lord to Jeremiah that God had formed him in his mother's womb is sung in greater detail by one of the psalmists:

> For thou didst form my inward parts,
>   thou didst knit me together in my mother's womb.
> I praise thee, for thou art fearful and wonderful.
>   Wonderful are thy works!
> Thou knowest me right well;
>   my frame was not hidden from thee,
> when I was being made in secret,
>   intricately wrought in the depths of the earth.
> Thy eyes beheld my unformed substance;
>   in thy book were written, every one of them,
> the days that were formed for me,
>   when as yet there was none of them.
>   (Ps. 139:13–16)

Other psalmists expressed their conviction that God had taken them from their mother's womb (Ps. 22:9f.; 71:6).

These, of course, are statements by those who felt themselves to be especially close to God.

Second Isaiah transferred to the nation what other
passages say of the righteous individual:

> But now hear, O Jacob my servant,
>   Israel whom I have chosen!
> Thus says the LORD who made you,
>   who formed you from the womb and will help you:
> Fear not, O Jacob my servant,
>   Jeshurun whom I have chosen.
>
> (Isa. 44:1f.; see also 46:3f.)

This prophet also used conception and birth as similes to
convey the unqualified sovereignty of God:

> Woe to him who says to a father, "What are you
>   begetting?"
> or to a woman, "With what are you in travail?"
> Thus says the LORD,
>   the Holy One of Israel, and his Maker:
> "Will you question me about my children,
>   or command me concerning the work of my hands?"
>
> (Isa. 45:10f.)

The laws reserving the firstborn to the Lord may have
their rationale in the primacy of God's role in conception
and birth. An early law declares, "The LORD said to
Moses, 'Consecrate to me all the first-born; whatever is
the first to open the womb among the people of Israel,
both of man and of beast, is mine' " (Ex. 13:1; see also
ch. 34:19f. and Num. 8:16–18 for a later witness). Johannes Pedersen explained the sacrifice of the first produce of orchards and fields and the firstborn of woman
and beast in these words: "When something alien is to
be absorbed [into the life of the holy people], it must be
sanctified, Yahweh being given his share; in this way it is
prepared for appropriation by the special Israelite psy-
che."[30] This may be the correct explanation. It also is

possible that the return to Yahweh of the first life to come from womb and field was a thank-offering to celebrate God's gift of all subsequent life through that source.

The material we have just reviewed is of such importance for understanding the status of woman in the Old Testament that we need to describe its significance carefully. Earlier in this chapter it was noted that a functional differentiation between the sexes in ancient Israel assigned to the male the formal transmission of the family's name and to the female the bearing of new life. The information just reviewed places the role of the female in its context. New life was held to be the result of a continuing divine activity which took place in conception, the growth of the fetus, and in the opening of the womb.

Thus, although the promise of progeny and name was given the whole people and was recorded as transmitted through the father, the divine presence and activity which guaranteed the progeny was resident in the woman. Her fecundity was the most crucial and clearest proof of God's presence in the midst of the people. The birth of children was testimony to God's continued care for the people.

This statement of the place of woman in ancient Israel seems so basic that I feel justified in turning to it, rather than to an anthropological construct, for the understanding of the significance of the patriarchal traits of Israelite society for the status of woman. This will be discussed later.

IV

Husbands and wives shared responsibility for the rearing of children. A description of the woman's role must not, therefore, be taken to prove that women alone cared for their offspring.

In dealing with something as universal as the relationship of children to parents, we see how pointless it is to claim for a single part of our heritage a decisive role in the formation of our family ideal. What can be noted, however, is the striking way in which reports of an ancient Israelite mother's relationships with her child are intelligible to us. It is this universality which has made the story of Solomon's judgments between two harlots so well known. Each woman, we are told, had just given birth to a child. One of them accidentally suffocated hers during the night. When she discovered it, she exchanged her dead infant for the living infant of her sleeping roommate. One woman accused the other of having changed babies, the charge was denied, and the matter came to Solomon for resolution. His solution to the problem was based upon the conviction that mother love is strong and selfless:

> And the king said, "Bring me a sword." So a sword was brought before the king. And the king said, "Divide the living child in two, and give half to the one, and half to the other." Then the woman whose son was alive said to the king, because her heart yearned for her son, "Oh, my lord, give her the living child, and by no means slay it." But the other said, "It shall be neither mine nor yours; divide it." Then the king answered and said, "Give the living child to the first woman, and by no means slay it; she is its mother." (I Kings 3:24–27)

Less graphic but equally universal in its appeal is the sage's evocation of the mother's love for child when he said:

> When I was a son with my father,
>   tender, the only one in the sight of my mother. . . .
>   (Prov. 4:3)

A more somber story of maternal love is recorded in the account of the expulsion of Hagar at Sarah's demand after the birth of a son to Sarah. Hagar and her son were sent away with what bread and water she could carry.

> When the water in the skin was gone, she cast the child under one of the bushes. Then she went, and sat down over against him a good way off, about the distance of a bowshot; for she said, "Let me not look upon the death of the child." And as she sat over against him, the child lifted up his voice and wept. (Gen. 21:15f.)

Those who know the terrible heat and dryness of the desert find this far too vivid.

Oddly enough, we are given few details of a mother's care for her children. Mothers seem to have traveled with their children (Gen. 33:1f.), sometimes in wagons (Gen. 45:19; 46:5). Hannah made Samuel's clothing and brought it with her each year when she came to Shiloh with her husband (I Sam. 2:19).

An interesting report of a mother's care for a son is given in the account of Solomon's rise to the throne. When it had become clear that David had become senile, Bathsheba, acting on the advice of the prophet Nathan, went to David and said:

> My lord, you swore to your maidservant by the LORD your God, saying, "Solomon your son shall reign after me, and he shall sit upon my throne." And now, behold, Adonijah is king, although you, my lord the king, do not know it. He has sacrificed oxen, fatlings, and sheep in abundance, and has invited all the sons of the king, Abiathar the priest, and Joab the commander of the army; but Solomon your servant he has not invited. And now, my lord the king, the eyes of all Israel are upon you, to tell them who shall sit on the throne of my lord the king after him. Otherwise it will come to pass, when my lord the king sleeps with his fathers, that I and my son Solomon will be counted offenders. (I Kings 1:17–21)

No sooner had she finished than Nathan arrived to reiterate her message (vs. 22–27). David then did precisely what the conspirators desired. He proclaimed Solomon king (vs. 28–30). We do not know whether David had earlier promised Bathsheba that Solomon would succeed him, but the presence of collusion between Nathan and Bathsheba and their manipulation of the emotions of the aged king are clear.

The tribute of the Old Testament to maternal love, and to the care of mothers for their children, is graphically displayed in similes. So crucial was a mother's love that it became an obvious analogy for the relationship between the Lord and Israel. Thus Second Isaiah proclaimed the continuing love of the Lord for the exiled people of Israel:

> But Zion said, "The LORD has forsaken me,
>   my Lord has forgotten me."
> "Can a woman forget her sucking child,
>   that she should have no compassion on the son
>   of her womb?
> Even these may forget,
>   yet I will not forget you.
> Behold, I have graven you on the palms of my hands;
>   your walls are continually before me."
>   (Isa. 49:14–16; see also ch. 66:13)

The strength of ancient Israel's appreciation of the love of the mother for her children made it also a simile for divine judgment. In Deuteronomy, the attempt to convey the magnitude of the devastation of divine judgment produced this incredible passage:

> And you shall eat the offspring of your own body, the flesh of your sons and daughters, whom the LORD your God has given you, in the siege and in the distress with which your enemies shall distress you. The man who is the most tender and delicately bred among you will grudge food to his brother, to the wife of his bosom, and to the last of the children who remain to him; so that he will not give to any

of them any of the flesh of his children whom he is eating, because he has nothing left to him, in the siege and in the distress with which your enemy shall distress you in all your towns. The most tender and delicately bred woman among you, who would not venture to set the sole of her foot upon the ground because she is so delicate and tender, will grudge to the husband of her bosom, to her son and to her daughter, her afterbirth that comes out from between her feet and her children whom she bears, because she will eat them secretly, for want of all things, in the siege and in the distress with which your enemy shall distress you in your towns. (Deut. 28:53-57)

II Kings 6:28f. (and Lam. 2:20; 4:10) make it clear that the Deuteronomic writer was not the victim of an over-heated imagination. When we realize the almost unimag-inable extremities which were always a possibility in the lives of the ancient Israelites, we finally see that Hosea's bitter words may have been a prayer for the only divine mercy possible in extremity:

> Give them, O LORD—
> what wilt thou give?
> Give them a miscarrying womb
> and dry breasts.
>
> (Hos. 9:14)

V

The material in this chapter is decisive for the under-standing of the status of woman in the Old Testament. It has been suggested that survival was the primary con-cern of a society forced to cope with disease, famine, and incessant war. In their social organization, the ancient Israelites assigned to the male the formal preservation of the basic structure of the society, the family; but to the female belonged the constant replenishment of the pool

of life that was the guarantor of the survival of the group.
Because they believed passionately that God had promised them survival if they were faithful to God, and because they saw all new life to be the consequence of the
Lord's direct intervention, the woman was seen to be a
primary locus of divine activity. Her fecundity was a basic
evidence of divine care for Israel. Motherhood thus was
not only a biological and sociological function. It was a
sacred act of great magnitude which only the woman
could perform. The very high esteem in which the
mother was held was then described, especially as it is
reflected in similes of God's care for Israel and of God's
judgment upon Israel.

No higher status could be given anyone than was given
the mother in ancient Israel.

CHAPTER 5

The Subservience of Women

I

We turn in this chapter to the kinds of evidence that have often led students of the Old Testament to claim that women were wholly subordinate to men in ancient Israel. The data will be discussed under two major categories: ways in which the woman was subordinated to her father, and ways in which the woman was subordinated to her husband. As noted in a previous chapter, a brother might occupy the position of the father in a family when the father had died.

Women subject to the authority of the father fall into three classes: unmarried daughters, married daughters, and daughters-in-law. Evidence describing the third category is slight and comes from reports of the life of the so-called extended family. Since authority over daughters-in-law was essentially an extension of the father's authority over a married son, we shall eliminate it from our discussion. We shall be concerned only with the ways in which fathers could exercise authority over unmarried and married daughters.

II

A daughter's identity was defined to a significant degree by the role of her father. An unmarried daughter of a priest could eat those parts of the sacrifice reserved for the priest:

> But the breast that is waved and the thigh that is offered you shall eat in any clean place, you and your sons and your daughters with you; for they are given as your due and your sons' due, from the sacrifices of the peace offerings of the people of Israel. (Lev. 10:14; see also Num. 18:8–14)

So also could a priest's childless daughter who was widowed or divorced (Lev. 22:13). The king's daughters were so important that they were listed separately in a tally of refugees fleeing to Egypt after the destruction of Jerusalem (Jer. 41:10; 43:5–7). This may be a reminder that the royal line might survive in exile through the daughters of the king.

If we assume that such commandments as "Honor your father and your mother" (Deut. 5:16) applied as much to daughters as to sons, we may conclude that daughters were ordered to obey their parents. We will find ample evidence in the next chapter to support the conclusion that sons were expected to obey their mothers. Relatively little, however, is said explicitly about daughters obeying their fathers. All the passages to be cited on this point are post-exilic.

The Chronicler reported that the seventeen sons and daughters of Haman served under him as Temple musicians (I Chron. 25:5f.). Shallum, son of Hallohesh, lived in Jerusalem after the exile, and he and his daughters helped rebuild the walls of the city (Neh. 3:12). Apparently the girls were sturdy!

The primary Old Testament example of an obedient daughter is Esther. This is all the more impressive since her parents were dead and Mordecai had taken their place. The theme of her obedience is introduced early in the book: "Now Esther had not made known her kindred or her people, as Mordecai had charged her; for Esther obeyed Mordecai just as when she was brought up by him" (Esth. 2:20). After she had become queen, each of her increasingly important decisions was taken only after consultation with him.

A series of passages, several of them quite ancient, indicate that the father had the authority to dispose of his daughter in several different ways. We have already reviewed the father's giving his daughter in marriage.[31] I Chronicles 2:34f. gives an additional example. Sheshan, who had daughters but no sons, gave one of his daughters to an Egyptian slave who may then have taken his father-in-law's name (see Ezra 2:61; Neh. 7:63) to ensure the preservation of the family line. The right of the father to refuse to give his unbetrothed daughter to her seducer even though the seducer had given "the marriage present for virgins" (Ex. 22:16f.) may reflect the father's right to withhold his family's participation in the building up of the family of a criminal. In both of these instances, the father seems to have been acting as the titular head of the family and on its behalf. So also, essentially, was the poor father who sold a daughter to become a slave wife, i.e., a concubine (Ex. 21:7–11).

Three passages report a father's disposition of a daughter in an especially repugnant manner. The first is the story of the destruction of Sodom and Gomorrah. Lot, who was living in Sodom, had three strangers visit him:

> But before they lay down, the men of the city, the men of Sodom, both young and old, all the people to the last man,

> surrounded the house; and they called to Lot, "Where are
> the men who came to you tonight? Bring them out to us, that
> we may know them." Lot went out of the door to the men,
> shut the door after him, and said, "I beg you, my brothers,
> do not act so wickedly. Behold, I have two daughters who
> have not known man; let me bring them out to you, and do
> to them as you please; only do nothing to these men, for they
> have come under the shelter of my roof." (Gen. 19:4–8)

Here, as often elsewhere, the verb "to know" means to
have sexual relations with. A similar situation is reported
in Judg. 19:22–24.

The third passage is the story of Jephthah's sacrifice
of his daughter. During a campaign in which Jephthah
led the Gileadites against the Ammonites, he vowed to
sacrifice "whoever comes forth from the doors of my
house to meet me, when I return victorious from the
Ammonites" (Judg. 11:31). He was greeted by his daughter, his only child.

> And when he saw her, he rent his clothes, and said, "Alas,
> my daughter! you have brought me very low, and you have
> become the cause of great trouble to me; for I have opened
> my mouth to the LORD, and I cannot take back my vow." And
> she said to him, "My father, if you have opened your mouth
> to the LORD, do to me according to what has gone forth from
> your mouth, now that the LORD has avenged you on your
> enemies, on the Ammonites." (Judg. 11:35–36)

She requested only that she be allowed three months to
"wander on the mountains, and bewail my virginity, I and
my companions." When she returned, she was sacrificed
(vs. 37–39). This narrative must be read in the light of the
strong condemnation of child sacrifice in the Deuteronomic law code and history (Deut. 12:30f.; 18:
9–12; II Kings 17:17).

The story of the sacrifice of Jephthah's daughter in

Judg. 11:34–40 may have been a legend explaining an annual rite in which young women mourned for those of their number who had died before they had "known a man," that is, before they had had the opportunity to fulfill their unique, sacred role in Israel. The sharp condemnation of child sacrifice by the Deuteronomists, and their identification of it as a cult act in the religions of Israel's neighbors, indicate that the ancient Israelite father did not have the right to sacrifice a daughter or son. This tends to be confirmed by the narrative in which Abraham is given a substitute, a ram, when attempting to sacrifice his son (Gen. 22:1–14). It also may suggest that the legend of Jephthah's daughter may have been non-Israelite in origin.

Many other reports of relationships between daughters and fathers reflect the primacy and structure of the Israelite family. As we will see when passages alluding to widows are discussed, it was a major misfortune for anyone not to be part of a family group. For this reason, a divorced wife returned to the family of her father (Lev. 22:13; Num. 18:19). Since the father was the titular head of the family, he could make vows which were binding upon the entire household, as Jeremiah found when he tested the faithfulness of the Rechabites to their vows by offering them wine. They rejected the wine, saying, "We have obeyed the voice of Jonadab the son of Rechab, our father, in all that he commanded us, to drink no wine all our days, ourselves, our wives, our sons, or our daughters" (Jer. 35:8).

Similarly, daughters shared in the punishment or blessing experienced by the family. The inclusiveness of the family circle is tersely described in an oracle of judgment pronounced by Jeremiah: "But from our youth the shameful thing has devoured all for which our fathers labored, their flocks and their herds, their sons and their daughters."[32] Daughters and sons also were included in predictions of the restoration of the people, as in Isa. 60:4:

> Lift up your eyes round about, and see;
>> they all gather together, they come to you;
> your sons shall come from far,
>> and your daughters shall be carried in the arms.

See also Zech. 8:4f. and 9:16f.

Passages of this type have rarely been listed as examples of the father exercising authority over the family because the individualism that permeates our culture makes it difficult for us to appreciate the corporately oriented culture of ancient Israel. The Israelite family lived far more as a unit than do we. The father, the titular head of the ancient Israelite family, was more a personification of the whole family than an individual who ruled it. The conduct of the family as a whole was described as his conduct, and the results of that conduct were experienced by the family as a whole. Thus the inclusion of daughters and sons in punishment for fathers' sins illuminates the true nature of the father's authority over the family. It also records a sociological reality with which we attempt to cope when we try to break self-perpetuating cycles of ignorance, malnutrition, and intergroup hostility. As is often the case, it is the sages who describe tersely and wryly something said more fully elsewhere in the Old Testament:

> The leech has two daughters;
> "Give, give," they cry.
>   (Prov. 30:15a)

We say, "Like father, like son."

What has just been said about individuals in the family also must be said about families in the clan, tribe, and the people of God. The ban on the sacrifice of daughters and sons just reported is imposed upon the father as the personification of the family because the family is part of the people of a deity who prohibits such conduct. The priest was the personification of the people of the Lord in certain cultic relationships with deity. Therefore, "the daughter of any priest, if she profanes herself by playing the harlot, profanes her father; she shall be burned with fire" (Lev. 21:9). Leviticus 19:29 extends to every family which is a part of the people covenanted with the Lord what was said of the daughter of a priest: "Do not profane your daughter by making her a harlot, lest the land fall into harlotry and the land become full of wickedness." Here the parents are prohibited from doing something to a daughter that would make her, and through her her family, offensive to God.

Parents continued to exercise enough authority over married daughters to give them some protection against their husbands. This is most clear in two areas: in the parents' defense of their daughter's nuptial chastity, and in the father's power to make void a daughter's marriage.

The first of these parental roles is described in Deut. 22:13–21:

> If any man takes a wife, and goes in to her, and then spurns her, and charges her with shameful conduct, and brings an evil name upon her, saying, "I took this woman, and when I came near her, I did not find in her the tokens of virginity," then the father of the young woman and her mother shall take and bring out the tokens of her virginity to the elders of the city in the gate; and the father of the young woman shall say to the elders, "I gave my daughter to this man to wife, and he spurns her; and lo, he has made shameful charges against her, saying, 'I did not find in your daughter the tokens of virginity,' and yet these are the tokens of my daughter's virginity." And they shall spread the garment before the elders of the city. Then the elders of that city shall take the man and whip him; and they shall fine him a hun-

dred shekels of silver, and give them to the father of the young woman, because he has brought an evil name upon a virgin of Israel; and she shall be his wife; he may not put her away all his days. But if the thing is true, that the tokens of virginity were not found in the young woman, then they shall bring out the young woman to the door of her father's house, and the men of her city shall stone her to death with stones, because she has wrought folly in Israel by playing the harlot in her father's house; so you shall purge the evil from the midst of you.

The implications of Deut. 22:13–21 are many. We are concerned here with three. If the husband's charge against the bride were true, it would not only deny to her the opportunity to perform her basic role in society (bearing children), it also would cost her her life. Such an accusation, therefore, was very grave. Secondly, the charge was a charge against the bride's family and was dealt with as such. The parents assumed the responsibility for the bride's defense. Should she be proved guilty, her crime was against "her father's house." The implication is that she had made her father's house untruthful because its words did not agree with its deeds. Finally, a successful parental defense of the daughter's virginity strengthened both families at the same time that it penalized the husband for a malicious charge. The bride's family received an even greater recompense for the loss of the daughter, and the family being established by the unhappy couple is guaranteed the possibility of children. This law must be read in the light of other laws quoted here earlier in which the wife's conjugal rights included not only support but sexual access to the husband (see Gen. 30:14–16; Ex. 21:10).

The second way in which a father could protect a married daughter's rights was through his power to declare a marriage void. There are only two reports of this, neither of them in the form of a legal prescription. One of these is a minor motif in the Samson legend. When Samson sought to cohabit with his Philistine wife from whom he had absented himself for some time, her father prevented it, saying, "I really thought that you utterly hated her; so I gave her to your companion" (Judg. 15:2). The notation in David's marital history is equally brief and matter-of-fact: "Saul had given Michal his daughter, David's wife, to Palti the son of Laish, who was of Gallim" (I Sam. 25:43f.).

Much is said in the literature on Hebrew marriage about the unfettered right of the husband to secure a divorce, and Judg. 15:2 may reflect that situation. Samson's father-in-law seems simply to have concluded that Samson had divorced his daughter and to have acted on that assumption by giving her in marriage to another suitor. The report of Saul's action is a different matter. As the composite narrative in I Samuel now flows, David had become an outlaw after his marriage to Michal. Thereupon Saul voided his daughter's marriage and gave her in marriage to another. It would seem likely that Saul had acted to free his daughter from an unsuitable marriage.

Each of these incidents, but especially the second, will need to be borne in mind when divorce is discussed. Too much may have been made in the past of the husband's apparently exclusive right to secure a divorce. These passages indicate that securing a divorce may actually have been one of the functions of the head of a family. The husband, as head of a family, could divorce his wife. The evidence is clear on this. But the father, as head of a family, seems also to have been able to secure a divorce for a daughter. Her rights in marriage continued to be protected by her family. This is the intention of the warning Laban gave Jacob, the husband of his two daughters, when he and Jacob parted company: "If you ill-treat my daughters . . . although no man is with us, remember,

God is witness between you and me" (Gen. 31:50).

We have already noted an instance in which the husband took the family name of his wife, presumably when his father-in-law had no son to preserve the family name (Ezra 2:61; Neh. 7:63). When such an arrangement existed in the extended family, the father of the married daughter seems to have exercised a father's authority over his son-in-law also. This appears to be the situation behind Lot's attempt to persuade the men betrothed to his daughters to leave Sodom with him, since Lot seems to have had no sons. When they refused to go, Lot, accompanied by his wife and daughters, left without them (Gen. 19:12–16). This, of course, ended the betrothals.

III

The relationship between husband and wife receives far more attention in the Old Testament than the one between daughter and father.

The wife is identified as a part of the household in stories about the patriarchs,[33] in law codes, and in both early and late narratives (I Sam. 30:1–25; Dan. 5:2, 23). Exodus 20:17 is one of the best-known examples of this: "You shall not covet your neighbor's house; you shall not covet your neighbor's wife, or his manservant, or his maidservant, or his ox, or his ass, or anything that is your neighbor's." The wife here is the first-named member of the household. She is not listed as property, as is so often thought. The wife is named before the household in the Deuteronomic parallel (Deut. 5:21), a change that indicates her standing even more clearly.

The Chronicler, writing in the late post-exilic period, continued the practice of identifying the wife as a part of the household by such notations as, "The priests were enrolled with all their little children, their wives, their sons, and their daughters, the whole multitude" (II Chron. 31:18). The identification of a woman in the royal harem with her husband meant that sexual access to her by someone else, either during the king's lifetime or after his death, established a claim to the throne. Adonijah, Solomon's older brother, asked for David's youngest concubine after Solomon's coronation. Solomon replied to his mother, who had transmitted Adonijah's request, "And why do you ask Abishag the Shunammite for Adonijah? Ask for him the kingdom also; for he is my elder brother, and on his side are Abiathar the priest and Joab the son of Zeruiah" (I Kings 2:22). The attempt to establish a claim to the throne by cohabiting with a member of a king's harem is probably the reason for Abner's going in to Rizpah, the dead Saul's concubine (II Sam. 3:6–11), and for Absalom's lying with members of David's harem during Absalom's revolt against David (II Sam. 16:20–22). The ancient Israelites felt that consorts of a king had become contagious. Sexual contact with them could convey royal power.

The closeness of the union of husband and wife was not necessarily true of slaves. The married Israelite who became a slave took his wife with him when he became free after his service, but a wife given him when he was a slave remained the property of his master. His only alternative under such circumstances was to bind himself to the master in perpetuity or to leave his slave wife behind (Ex. 21:2–6).

Another series of passages suggest that the husband owned his wife. The thematic statement of this, so to speak, has been quoted here before. It is the curse on the woman in the Garden of Eden:

> To the woman he [God] said,
> "I will greatly multiply your pain in childbearing;
>   in pain you shall bring forth children,
> yet your desire shall be for your husband,
>   and he shall rule over you."
>
> (Gen. 3:16)

The force of the final line of this passage should not be discounted because it seems to stand alone in the Old Testament. To it should be added all those passages in which the Hebrew root *b'l* is to be translated either "to marry" when it appears as a verb or as "husband" when it is a noun.[34] The same root also means, more frequently, "to rule over" as a verb and "lord" or "master" as a noun.

Genesis 3:16 and the primary meaning of the root *b'l* have been taken to be adequate proof that the Israelite husband owned, or ruled, his wife.[35] The force of the argument becomes much less convincing, however, when Gen. 3:16 is given the meaning assigned it here earlier (Chapter 2), and when we seek instances in which husbands acted toward their wives in ways that we would take to express their rule over the wives.

We are given four reports of a husband making his wife sexually available to others. This custom, if it did exist, would constitute in our eyes a display of authority as absolute as it is offensive. The four passages are Gen. 12:10–20; 20:1–18; 26:6–11; and Judg. 19:1–29. In the first three of these, a husband (Abraham twice, Isaac once) lets another marry his wife whom he has claimed to be a sister for his own safety's sake while living in a foreign land. The fourth tells of a Levite, a visitor in Gibeah, who thrust his concubine outside to entertain the men of Gibeah seeking homosexual relations with him. In each passage, the theme arises out of the dramatic necessity of the story being told. There are no references to such a male prerogative in any other narrative, or in laws confirming, limiting, or denying the right.

Genesis 12:10–20 contains one of the devices by means of which the author heightens the dramatic tension arising out of the Lord's promise of descendants to Abraham, the eponymous ancestor of Israel. No heir can be born if the marriage be broken (just as there can be no heir if the wife be barren). The story is given a second time in the E stratum (Gen. 20:1–18), with the explanation that Abraham and Sarah had the same father but not the same mother (v. 12). This mitigates the scandal of Abraham's conduct slightly. The tale serves the same purpose in both J and E. A similar incident is told of Isaac in Gen. 26:6–11, where the theme again is the faithfulness of the Lord in keeping promises to the patriarchs in spite of great obstacles. It seems quite probable that the thrice-told story is a theological statement about the faithfulness of God in covenantal promises rather than a description of a husband's rights over his wife, and that the faithfulness of the Lord is underscored by telling about it in a context in which the patriarchs themselves had acted reprehensibly.

Judges 19:1–29 is a grim story. The concubine of a Levite living in Ephraim fled to her father's home in Judah. The Levite, following her, retrieved her. Returning to his home in the north, he stopped for the night in Gibeah of Benjamin. As he and his host visited, the men of the village gathered outside and said to the host, "Bring out the man who came into your house, that we may know him" (v. 22). The host offered his daughter and the Levite's concubine in place of the Levite (vs. 23f.):

> But the men would not listen to him. So the man seized his concubine, and put her out to them; and they knew her, and abused her all night until the morning. And as the dawn began to break, they let her go. And as morning appeared,

the woman came and fell down at the door of the man's house where her master was, till it was light. And her master rose up in the morning, and when he opened the doors of the house and went out to go on his way, behold, there was his concubine lying at the door of the house, with her hands on the threshold. He said to her, "Get up, let us be going." But there was no answer. Then he put her upon the ass; and the man rose up and went away to his home. (Vs. 25–28)

In the sequel, the Levite carved up his concubine's corpse and sent a piece to each of the tribes of Israel, asking vengeance on the men of Gibeah (vs. 29f.). All Israel responded except the tribe of Benjamin. It chose to defend a village within its borders (ch. 20:1–17). A civil war followed in which the tribe of Benjamin would have been exterminated had not their former enemies allowed them to capture wives for themselves from the maidens celebrating a vintage festival at Shiloh (chs. 20:18 to 21: 24).

Judges, chs. 19 to 21, is a confused narrative. Our concern is primarily with ch. 19:25–29, which seems to provide proof that the male head of the family could make a daughter or wife available sexually to strangers outside marriage.

A different view of the meaning of Judg. 19:25–29 emerges from a study of comparisons with the accounts of the sinfulness of the men of Sodom (Gen. 19:1–11) and of the rise of Saul to the throne (I Sam. 11:1–11).[36] The homosexual demands of the men of Gibeah parallel the demands of the men of Sodom (Judg. 19:22 = Gen. 19:5); the host is not a native of the community (Judg. 19:16 = Gen. 19:9); the host offers a daughter (or daughters) in place of the guest (or guests) (Judg. 19:24 = Gen. 19:8); the host calls the conduct of the men of the town depraved (Judg. 19:23 = Gen. 19:7); and action by the guest (or guests) resolves the crisis (Judg. 19:25 = Gen. 19:10). Gibeah of Benjamin is the locale of the crime reported in Judg. 19:25–28 and the home of Saul (I Sam. 11:4f.); the Levite and Saul respond to violence by sending a chunk of flesh to each tribe with a summons to assemble (Judg. 19:29 = I Sam. 11:7); and all Israel is said to have responded (Judg. 20:1 = I Sam. 11:8).

These comparisons suggest the following conclusions: The odium of the reputation of the men of Sodom is being extended to the men of Gibeah, the most prominent of whom was Saul, the first king of Israel; and the odium of the reputation of Lot (Gen. 19:30–38) is being extended to the sojourner in Gibeah and to the Levite. Thus we probably should conclude that all actions reported in Judg., ch. 19—except the offer of hospitality— were viewed by narrator and hearers as evil. The story gained its effectiveness from the immorality and illegality of the power exercised by father and husband. Judges, ch. 19, provided a bridge between the story of Sodom and the account of the rise of Saul to the throne, conveying the evil repute of the Sodomites to Saul. So understood, the chapter becomes another example of the polemic of the Davidic historians against the earlier dynasty established by Saul. Even the role of the Levite conforms to this interpretation. By the time of Solomon, David's son and heir, the levitical priesthood had largely been displaced in royal favor by the Zadokites, a hereditary Jerusalemite priesthood. It is probably no accident that the Levite is described as refusing to stay for the night in Jerusalem (vs. 10–12)! If these conclusions be valid, we cannot use Judg. 19:23–29 as a report of the rights of father over daughter and husband over wife.

Other instances of the authority of an Israelite husband over a wife are rare and easily described. The vows of Rechabites to follow a nomadic life bound every member of the family, including the wife (Jer. 35:8–10), and the husband could, within limits to be described later, countermand vows made by his wife (Num. 30:6–15). No reports of husbands voiding their wives' vows have survived, however. The relationship between Ahasuerus and Vashti and Esther, described in The Book of Esther, reflects the author's understanding of the authority of a royal Persian husband over his harem, whether that picture is historically accurate or not. It may be significant that Esther, the Jewish woman, is pictured as more obedient than Vashti, the Persian.

One notation at the end of the account of Absalom's revolt against David seems to be historical:

> And David came to his house at Jerusalem; and the king took the ten concubines whom he had left to care for the house, and put them in a house under guard, and provided for them, but did not go in to them. So they were shut up until the day of their death, living as if in widowhood. (II Sam. 20:3)

These were the royal concubines with whom Absalom cohabited during his attempt to usurp David's throne. The narrative seems to reflect the strictures surrounding the royal family more than the authority of the average husband over a wife.

Thus the search for examples of an exercise of authority by the husband over a wife who was a freewoman really contributes only the information that a husband could make void a wife's vow (as also could a father void an unmarried daughter's vow). Beyond this, there is surprisingly little: the statement in Gen. 3:16 and the contrast between Queen Vashti and Esther. This is not enough evidence to sustain the picture of the husband as tyrant over the wife. In the end, therefore, the real basis for that picture is the use of the term *ba'al* both as husband and as lord. In a culture in which corporate identity took precedence over individual identity, it is likely that the individual whom we would identify as an authority figure was viewed as a personification of the group. This means that we almost certainly misunderstand the meaning of *ba'al* when we define it in terms of authority.

Other descriptions of the relationship between female and male in marriage picture them either as being treated alike or as sharing a common life, whether for good or ill.

Adultery and rape are dealt with under four categories in the laws of the Old Testament. The first is a prescription for the trial by ordeal for a wife accused of secret adultery (Num. 5:11–31). Should the wife be guilty of the charge, the potion she drinks under priestly supervision will "cause bitter pain, and her body shall swell, and her thigh shall fall away, and the woman shall become an execration among her people" (v. 27). If she be innocent, however, none of this will happen. Instead, "if the woman has not defiled herself and is clean, then she shall be free and shall conceive children" (v. 28). Evidence is slowly accumulating which attests to the effectiveness of such trials by ordeal in a culture in which they are accepted as valid.[37]

The second category is adultery in which the participants are caught in the act. Here, the Deuteronomic law dealt with both man and woman in the same way: "If a man is found lying with the wife of another man, both of them shall die, the man who lay with the woman, and the woman; so you shall purge the evil from Israel" (Deut. 22:22). The severity of the punishment becomes more understandable when we remember that the ancient Israelites regarded conception, pregnancy, and birth as the result of God acting in the woman after the cohabitation of female and male. Adultery is often described as a violation of another man's property rights,[38] a position which simply does not account for the Israelite belief about the role of God in establishing and perpetuating families. This punishment is prescribed for all major offenses against God in the Old Testament.

The third and fourth categories deal with two forms of rape, each one the violation of a betrothed maiden. If the incident takes place in a town or village, it is treated as adultery and both are to be stoned, "the young woman because she did not cry for help though she was in the city, and the man because he violated his neighbor's wife" (Deut. 22:24b). If the rape happened in the open country, however, only the man was executed "because he came upon her in the open country, and though the betrothed young woman cried for help there was no one to rescue her" (Deut. 22:27). In each of these instances, a betrothed woman is viewed in law as married. Thus man and woman were treated alike in cases of known adultery, but with one exception. When the greater physical strength of the male may have been used without the female having the means to resist, only the male was punished.

Husbands and wives also were as one when the people were held to be suffering punishment for sin. The way this is expressed conveys the impression at times that the wives will suffer for the sins of their husbands, as in a woe against a priest at Bethel who tried to hinder Amos from prophesying:

Now therefore hear the word of the LORD.
You say, "Do not prophesy against Israel,
    and do not preach against the house of Isaac."
Therefore thus says the LORD:
"Your wife shall be a harlot in the city,
    and your sons and your daughters shall fall by the
        sword,
    and your land shall be parceled out by line;
you yourself shall die in an unclean land,
    and Israel shall surely go into exile away from its
        land."

(Amos 7:16f.)

The priest, however, spoke for a cultic community of which he, his family, and the court were a part (see Amos 7:10–13),[39] and the punishment described by Amos was to fall upon the entire community. The corporateness of both offense and punishment is stated more clearly in Jer. 6:10–12:

> To whom shall I speak and give warning,
>   that they may hear?
> Behold, their ears are closed,
>   they cannot listen;
> behold, the word of the LORD is to them an object of scorn,
>   they take no pleasure in it.
> Therefore I am full of the wrath of the LORD;
>   I am weary of holding it in.
> "Pour it out upon the children in the street,
>   and upon the gatherings of young men, also;
> both husband and wife shall be taken,
>   the old folk and the very aged.
> Their houses shall be turned over to others,
>   their fields and wives together;
> for I will stretch out my hand
>   against the inhabitants of the land,"
>
> says the LORD.

The ways in which marital solidarity under punishment is described list most of the categories of suffering known to a people in antiquity which had experienced both natural disaster and defeat in war. Wives would be enslaved with their husbands (II Chron. 29:9), and queens and princesses would be taken into captivity with the king (II Kings 24:12, 15; Jer. 38:21–23). Wives would be killed (Hos. 13:16; Amos 4:1–3), raped (Deut. 28:30; Lam. 5:11), visited with plague (II Chron. 21:12–15), and widowed (Ps. 109:9).

The fusion of husband and wife into a single entity is reflected in the Old Testament in happier ways also. The industrious, economically independent wife in Prov. 31: 10–29 adds luster to her husband's standing among his peers:

> Her husband is known in the gates,
>   when he sits among the elders of the land.
>   (V. 23; see also Prov. 12:4)

Conversely, the qualities of the husband extended to his family. When the Queen of Sheba praised Solomon, she said: "Happy are your wives! Happy are these your servants, who continually stand before you and hear your wisdom!" (I Kings 10:8).

Thus it may be that the following description of judgment may have had a far greater impact than we might at first suspect. It describes divine punishment as the disintegration of the corporate fabric in which all persons found their identity:

> Put no trust in a neighbor,
>   have no confidence in a friend;
> guard the doors of your mouth
>   from her who lies in your bosom;
> for the son treats the father with contempt,
>   the daughter rises up against her mother,
> the daughter-in-law against her mother-in-law;
>   a man's enemies are the men of his own house.
>   (Micah 7:5f.)

IV

It is clear by this time that the conclusions we reach after viewing evidence in the Old Testament bearing on the status of woman are strongly influenced by our point of departure. Those who have begun with the presumption that the ancient Israelites lived in an authoritarian patriarchal social order have documented their case heavily. The same Biblical evidence, as well as some data ignored or little used, is being employed here to document a different reconstruction of the status of woman in the Old Testament. The point of departure here has been the ancient Israelite's belief that God worked in conception, pregnancy, and giving birth to create and sustain a people. We have been forced by this point of departure to magnify the status of woman, to see the role of the male as essentially complementary and supportive, and to provide an explanation of the evidence describing the relationships between the sexes which is an alternative to a now untenable traditional paternalistic view.

There is a large body of material that has never been intelligible from a patriarchal orientation. Much of it has been ignored. Some of it has been explained away. All of it, however, fits into the position being described here. This evidence falls broadly into two categories: instances in which a woman exercises authority within the family (in some cases, over her husband), and the quite varied activities of women outside the home. In the next chapter, we will examine evidence reporting the woman exercising authority within the home.

CHAPTER 6

Subservience to Women

I

Those in the household with whom the wife dealt were children, servants (including slaves), other wives, the husband, and the husband's parents.

Relationships between wives in a polygamous family seem to shed little light on the standing of woman in ancient Israel, and the evidence describing it is not presented here. The exception will be instances in which a wife who is a freewoman is relating to a wife who is a slave. This will be dealt with as the relationship of the wife to a slave. The implications of the existence of polygamy for the standing of women have already been discussed. The relationship between father-in-law and daughter-in-law, described only rarely in the Old Testament, was discussed in the last chapter. Also considered there were those cases in which the wife could be described as being subservient to the husband.

In this chapter, we will deal with the relationship between mother and child, the authority of the woman over servants (including slaves), and a group of passages in which the wife either seems to have a higher status than

the husband or appears to be exercising authority over
him.

II

The influence of a mother over her children is reflected in several passages in the Old Testament. When
the author of Judg., ch. 5, an ancient victory song, described the death of Sisera, the Canaanite commander,
he pictured Sisera's mother and not his wife as awaiting
his return with a bit of plunder for her (Judg. 5:28–30).
Abimelech, the only son of Gideon and a concubine,
appealed for the loyalty of the men of Shechem, his mother's home, on grounds of maternal kinship when he
and the other sons of Gideon sought to rule that city
(Judg. 9:1–3).

The Samson legends, also quite ancient, provide an
example of maternal influence that deserves to be
quoted:

> And Samson's wife wept before him, and said, "You only
> hate me, you do not love me; you have put a riddle to my
> countrymen, and you have not told me what it is." And he
> said to her, "Behold, I have not told my father nor my
> mother, and shall I tell you?" She wept before him the seven
> days that their feast lasted; and on the seventh day he told
> her, because she pressed him hard. Then she told the riddle
> to her countrymen. (Judg. 14:16f.)

Amusement with this picture should not blind us to the
hierarchy of relationships described. Samson initially rejected his wife's request because he saw no reason to tell
a wife something he had not yet told his father and
mother. The son's relationship to both parents was
closer than his tie with his wife. Nor are we told that the
wife resented Samson's bond with his parents, perhaps

because she was trying to betray him to the Philistines in order to save her father's house!

Solomon's respect for Bathsheba, his mother, is another illustration of the status of a mother in the eyes of her children. When Bathsheba entered the throne room, Solomon "rose to meet her, and bowed down to her; then he sat on his throne, and had a seat brought for the king's mother; and she sat on his right" (I Kings 2:19). Each of Solomon's movements reveals the extremely high status Bathsheba had in his eyes and in the mind of the one reporting the scene. He rose from his throne (the symbol of his royal power), bowed before her (an act of homage throughout the ancient Near East), and had her seated on his right (the position of honor).

Two songs that may have been used in weddings imply the high standing of a king's mother. One (Ps. 45:9) mentions the presence of the queen and describes her splendid robe. The second song attributes an act of major symbolic importance to the king's mother:

> Go forth, O daughters of Zion,
>   and behold King Solomon,
> with the crown with which his mother crowned him
>   on the day of his wedding,
>   on the day of the gladness of his heart.
>
> (S. of Sol. 3:11)

There are features of the Old Testament that continue to baffle scholars because so little is said about them either in the Scriptures themselves or in the literature of neighboring ancient Near Eastern peoples. Some of these cryptic references have been cleared up by archaeologists,[40] and this has encouraged students to believe that explanations eventually will be found for other examples. A case in point is the presence or absence of a reference to a king's mother in editorial summaries of reigns in the books of Kings and Chronicles. The data is given in tabular form on pages 92 and 93. No Biblical citation is given if the mother is not named.

Several comments can be made about this table. The first is that the names of the mothers of the sons of Josiah (Jehoahaz, Jehoiakim, and Zedekiah; Jehoiachin was a son of Jehoiakim) prove that Josiah had at least two wives. Jehoahaz' mother was Hamutal, who also bore Zedekiah. Jehoiakim's mother, however, was Zebidah. The second comment is that only one queen mother in the history of the Northern Kingdom (the Kingdom of Israel) is named—Zeruah, the mother of Jeroboam I. As was noted in a footnote to the chart, Jezebel was identified as the mother of Jehoram in a narrative but not in the editorial summaries with which we are dealing. The mother of Ahaziah, an older son of Ahab who preceeded Jehoram on the throne, is mentioned but not named. She may have been Jezebel. This is uncertain, however, since the size of Ahab's family requires a harem (II Kings 10:1). The mother of Ahaz, one of the kings of Judah, is neither mentioned nor named. Since Ahaz was the king who introduced the worship of an Assyrian god into the royal shrine in Jerusalem in place of the veneration of Yahweh (II Kings 16:10–16), it could reasonably be concluded that Ahaz' mother was ignored because he was judged to be evil. However, the Deuteronomic historian gives the name of the mother of Manasseh, a ruler condemned bell, book, and candle by that same historian (II Kings 21:2–16)! Furthermore, the Chronicler gives us the name of the mother of Rehoboam (the Deuteronomic historian does not), even though his folly was the immediate cause of the revolt of the northern tribes against the house of David. Finally, the Chronicler fails to name any queen mother after the reign of Hezekiah, even though all of them are identified in II Kings, the primary source used by the Chronicler.

It is difficult to provide a single explanation for the

TABLE COMPARING THE MENTION OF KINGS' MOTHERS
IN KINGS AND CHRONICLES

King of Judah	of Israel	Mother's Name	Books of Kings	Books of Chronicles
Rehoboam		Naamah		II Chron. 12:
	Jeroboam I	Zeruah	I Kings 11:26	
Abijam (Abijah)		Maacah	I Kings 15:1f.	
		Micaiah		II Chron. 13:
Asa		Maacah	I Kings 15:9f.	
	Nadab			
	Baasha			
	Elah			
	Zimri			
	Omri			
Jehoshaphat		Azubah	I Kings 22:41f.	II Chron. 20:
	Ahab			
	Ahaziah	*	I Kings 22:51f.	
	Jehoram (Joram)	**	II Kings 3:1f.	
Jehoram				
Ahaziah		Athaliah	II Kings 8:25f.	II Chron. 22
	Jehu			
Jehoash (Joash)		Zibiah	II Kings 12:1	II Chron. 24
	Jehoahaz			
	Jehoash (Joash)			
Amaziah		Jehoaddin	II Kings 14:1f.	
		Jehoaddan		II Chron. 25
	Jeroboam II			
Azariah (Uzziah)		Jecoliah	II Kings 15:1f.	II Chron. 26
	Zechariah			
	Shallum			
	Menahem			

Jotham		Jerusha	II Kings 15:32f.	II Chron. 27:1
	Pekahiah			
	Pekah			
Ahaz				
	Hoshea			
Hezekiah		Abi	II Kings 18:1f.	
		Abijah		II Chron. 29:1
Manasseh		Hephzibah	II Kings 21:1	
Amon		Meshullemeth	II Kings 21:19	
Josiah		Jedidah	II Kings 22:1	
Jehoahaz		Hamutal	II Kings 23:31	
Jehoiakim		Zebidah	II Kings 23:36	
Jehoiachin		Nehushta	II Kings 24:8	
Zedekiah		Hamutal	II Kings 24:18	

*Mother mentioned but not named.
**Mother (Jezebel) named elsewhere (II Kings 9:21-26).
The names of the mothers of Abijam (Abijah), Amaziah, and
Hezekiah differ slightly in Kings and Chronicles. Both forms of the
name are given, each with the appropriate citation.

evidence. The mere fact that so many of the queen mothers are named indicates that they were important. Their
status makes it likely that the failure to name them was
intentional. The most consistent pattern is the failure to
name the mothers of the kings of the Northern Kingdom.
This may be attributed fairly confidently to a defense of
the legitimacy of the claim of the Davidic dynasty to rule
all Israel. Jeroboam I's mother may have been named
because of the tradition that he was an adversary raised
up by the Lord to punish Solomon for his apostasies (I
Kings 11:9-13; 12:21-24).

It is possible that a second motive is present: queen
mothers were not named when the historians judged the
sons' reigns to be exceptionally evil. The Deuteronomic
historian does name Manasseh's mother even though he

condemns Manasseh strongly. It may be, however, that Manasseh's sins did not loom as large in the Deuteronomic historian's eyes as did those of Jehoram and Ahaz (both of whose mothers are ignored). The Chronicler so magnifies the reforms of Hezekiah that he makes them overshadow the reformation carried out later by Josiah, in contrast to the Deuteronomic historians who believed Josiah's reformation to be the greater. The consistent silence of the Chronicler after Hezekiah thus may be mute testimony to his view that all subsequent rulers had fallen away from the righteousness attributed to Hezekiah.

The naming of the queen mother seems to indicate her high standing in the kingdom.[41] We may also conclude, with some caution, that she was not named when the author held her influence to be evil as demonstrated by the conduct of her son. Each of these conclusions tends to be confirmed by additional evidence.

The importance of the queen mother is revealed more or less inadvertently in two incidents. The first is part of the report of Asa's reformation:

> And Asa did what was right in the eyes of the LORD, as David his father had done. He put away the male cult prostitutes out of the land, and removed all the idols that his fathers had made. He also removed Maacah his mother from being queen mother because she had an abominable image made for Asherah, and Asa cut down her image and burned it at the brook Kidron. (I Kings 15:11–13)

This was one of the steps, culminating in the reform of King Josiah, by means of which the worship of the Davidic court was gradually purged of its Canaanite traits. Maacah seems simply to have continued the kind of idolatry attributed also to Asa's "fathers." Her action must have carried so much weight that her reformer son had to destroy the idol she had caused to be put up and to demote her from her position in the court in order to carry out his reforms.

A second example is even more impressive. The reigns of the Davidides in Jerusalem were interrupted only once from the time that David captured the city until its destruction by the Babylonians in 586 B.C. The disruption came when Athaliah, a daughter of Ahab (and possibly of Jezebel), the queen mother in Jerusalem, seized the throne at the time of the death of Ahaziah her son and tried to have all of the males of the Davidic line killed:

> Now when Athaliah the mother of Ahaziah saw that her son was dead, she arose and destroyed all the royal family. But Jehosheba, the daughter of King Joram, sister of Ahaziah, took Joash the son of Ahaziah, and stole him away from among the king's sons who were about to be slain, and she put him and his nurse in a bedchamber. Thus she hid him from Athaliah, so that he was not slain; and he remained with her six years, hid in the house of the LORD, while Athaliah reigned over the land. (II Kings 11:1–3)

What was the basis of Athaliah's power? Even though she might have killed her grandsons herself, she alone could not have ruled the kingdom for six years. She seized the throne after her son Ahaziah, who had been visiting the king of Israel, had been killed during a revolt in the Northern Kingdom which destroyed all of Athaliah's family and its supporters (II Kings 9:16 to 10:12). The new ruler of Israel would hardly have supported her!

A part of the explanation probably lies in the personality of Athaliah. Even an imperious and able woman, however, would have needed some base upon which to build her seizure of the throne. The only one known to us would be the position held by the queen mother. Athaliah's revolt and her retention of the throne for six years suggests that the queen mother may have been even more powerful than the other evidence available to us would lead us to suspect.

Two passages in Jeremiah in which the king and his mother are linked in oracles of woe suggest that the queen mother may have been held accountable for the kind of king her son was. Both are addressed to Jehoia-chin and Nehushta, his mother, although she is not named.

> Say to the king and the queen mother:
> "Take a lowly seat,
> for your beautiful crown
>   has come down from your head."
> The cities of the Negeb are shut up,
>   with none to open them;
> all Judah is taken into exile,
>   wholly taken into exile.
>   (Jer. 13:18f.; see also ch. 22:26)

All the prophets, including Jeremiah, saw disasters present or pending as justly deserved punishment from the Lord. Thus the linking of mother and son in an oracle predicting disaster carries the implication that the mother was being held responsible for the kind of son she had reared.

This was said both of royal mothers and of the mothers of commoners. Saul's attack on Jonathan, when Jonathan displeased him, was, "You son of a perverse, rebellious woman, do I not know that you have chosen the son of Jesse to your own shame, and to the shame of your mother's nakedness?" (I Sam. 20:30b). Like mother, like son! Years later, when Jehu, the candidate of the prophetic party for the throne of Israel, met Joram, king of Israel and son of Ahab, Joram said: " 'Is it peace, Jehu?' He answered, 'What peace can there be, so long as the harlotries and the sorceries of your mother Jezebel are so many?' " (II Kings 9:22b). Once again, like mother, like son. What was held to be true of a relationship out of which came evil also was held to be true of a felicitous one.

> O LORD, I am thy servant;
> I am thy servant, the son of thy handmaid.
> Thou hast loosed my bonds.
>
> (Ps. 116:16)[42]

With the mother's responsibility for her son, of course, went the son's (or daughter's) responsibility for the mother. During his years of flight from Saul (or, perhaps more accurately, his years as a leader of a band of outlaws being pursued by Saul), David

> said to the king of Moab, "Pray let my father and my mother stay with you, till I know what God will do for me." And he left them with the king of Moab, and they stayed with him all the time that David was in the stronghold. (I Sam. 22:3b, 4)

The theme of The Book of Ruth has as one of its motifs the care given by Ruth, a young widow, for her widowed and bereaved mother-in-law (Ruth 2:11).

III

The bond between parents and children, and especially between mother and son, was so important in the fabric of ancient Israelite society that it became a recurring theme both in the wisdom literature and in the law codes.

Proverbs 31:1–9 is a brief, self-contained group of words of advice entitled "The words of Lemuel, king of Massa, which his mother taught him." It opens:

> What, my son? What, son of my womb?
> What, son of my vows?
>
> (Prov. 31:2)

This verse is difficult to translate. *The New English Bible* reads:

> "What, O my son, what shall I say to you,
> you, the child of my womb and answer to my prayers?"[43]

In either translation, the verse conveys a sense of the intimate bond between a son and the mother who instructed him.

Exhortations to heed parental instruction appear elsewhere in the book of The Proverbs:

> Hear, my son, your father's instruction,
>   and reject not your mother's teaching;
> for they are a fair garland for your head,
>   and pendants for your neck.
> (Prov. 1:8f.)

In reading Hebrew poetry, one is tempted to seek for a different meaning for each line. The basic structure of Hebrew poetry, however, is called parallelism. The two lines in each verse of this proverb, for example, parallel each other. In Prov. 10:1 the two lines are antithetical. The same content is conveyed in each statement:

> A wise son makes a glad father,
>   but a foolish son is a sorrow to his mother.

This proverb cannot be cited as evidence that the author believed the father could take credit for a wise son but a mother should be blamed for a foolish one. No contrast between the relationship of father and son, and mother and son, is intended. Husband and wife are given parity, as they are also in Prov. 17:25; 23:22; 28:24; 30:11f.

Even though the wisdom literature stresses the obligation of the sons to obey their parents, it does not neglect the responsibility of the parents to discipline the son:

The rod and reproof give wisdom,
but a child left to himself brings shame to his mother.
(Prov. 29:15)

Laws demanded what proverbs encouraged. The best-known statement of this appears in the Ten Commandments (Ex. 20:12; Deut. 5:16). Reverence for parents appears elsewhere also, however, as in Lev. 19:3: "Every one of you shall revere his mother and his father, and you shall keep my sabbaths: I am the LORD your God." In both the Ten Commandments and Lev. 19:3, more is asked than filial obedience. The son is to honor or to revere his father and mother. A fundamental attitude akin to religious veneration is urged from which more than simple obedience would result.

At the same time, other laws stipulated penalties for specific conduct as harsh as the punishment prescribed for offenses against God. Death was ordered for striking one's parents (Ex. 21:15), cursing father or mother (Ex. 21:17; Lev. 20:9; cf. Prov. 20:20), or disobedience (Deut. 21:18–21). A curse was taken very seriously. It was the attempt to harm another by supernatural agency. A curse on one's parents, therefore, was extremely grave. Even more serious would be such a communal curse on a wrongdoer as, "Cursed be he who dishonors his father or his mother" (Deut. 27:16a).

This is not the place to review the significance of the death penalty for violations of the covenant with God. It will have to suffice to say that the maintenance of a correct relationship with the diety upon whom the total life of the people depended was so crucial that extreme measures were believed to be justified in dealing with those who alienated God. The same severity of punishment appears in dealing with violations of the authority of parents over children. Thus the penalty prescribed in the laws just mentioned here is evidence of the importance for ancient Israelite society of the authority of the mother and father over the child. It also needs to be noted that there is no discrimination in favor of father and against mother. The mother's authority over the son is as great in the law codes as is that of the father.

By this time, we should have come to expect that a relationship as fundamental as that between mother and son would appear in similes. Such is the case. When the prophet Jeremiah tried to find a way to convey to others the anguish he felt when his proclamation of the word of the Lord was rejected, he said: "Woe is me, my mother, that you bore me, a man of strife and contention to the whole land! I have not lent, nor have I borrowed, yet all of them curse me" (Jer. 15:10). A psalmist, believing himself to be receiving evil from others in return for the good he had done them, described how he had lamented when they were ill, concluding:

> I went about as one who laments his mother,
>   bowed down and in mourning.
>
> (Ps. 35:14b)

The relationship between mother and son was used most often as a simile in the proclamation of judgment. The Second Isaiah likened Jerusalem to a bereaved mother (Isa. 51:18; see also v.20; Jer. 15:5–9):

> There is none to guide her
>   among all the sons she has borne;
> there is none to take her by the hand
>   among all the sons she has brought up.

The evidence available describing the influence of the mother over her sons, and thus the subservience of the sons to their mother, supports the conclusion that husband and wife shared the position of authority and its responsibilities. In many passages, particularly in laws and proverbs in which the self-conscious will of the society was carefully stated, no distinction is made between husband and wife. In the inadvertent witness so important to the historian, however, matters seem to be different. When the place of the queen mother is examined, it becomes clear that she occupied a unique and elevated position. Her husband, the king, had died, and a new king, her son, reigns. The son thus becomes the titular head of the family. But she to whom the king pays homage must have wielded great power and received widespread respect. The evidence supports this conclusion.

Royal families are distinctive and do not necessarily reflect the norm for the society as a whole. The royal family in ancient Israel seems to have remained polygamous even when the majority of the population was turning increasingly to monogamy, and the tie between mother and son in a polygamous family might have been closer than the mother-son bond in a monogamous marriage. For the latter, we have primarily the legal and proverbial statements which place husband and wife on an equal footing.

It is best in the end to conclude, therefore, that children were expected to be subservient to both mother and father. The wife was not inferior to the husband. In a polygamous marriage, she may have exercised more authority and have had more influence than did the father.

IV

The mistress exercised a good deal of authority over slaves. We are told several times that wives of the patriarchs made their personal female slaves their husbands' concubines. Sarai and Rachel did it when they were barren, and the child born to the slave could be counted to be the son of the mistress.

When Rachel saw that she bore Jacob no children, she envied her sister; and she said to Jacob, "Give me children, or I shall die!" Jacob's anger was kindled against Rachel, and he said, "Am I in the place of God, who has withheld from you the fruit of the womb?" Then she said, "Here is my maid Bilhah; go in to her, that she may bear upon my knees, and even I may have children through her." So she gave him her maid Bilhah as a wife; and Jacob went in to her. And Bilhah conceived and bore Jacob a son. Then Rachel said, "God has judged me, and has also heard my voice and given me a son"; therefore she called his name Dan [i.e., "He judged"]. (Gen. 30:1–6; on Sarai, see Gen. 16:1f.)

Since the number of children born to a woman increased her standing, a mother who had ceased bearing could assign her female slave to her husband and claim the issue as her own (Gen. 30:9–13).

Should the once-barren wife have a child after assigning her slave to her husband, a further demonstration of the wife's power over the slave became possible. We are told that Hagar, Sarai's slave, "looked with contempt" on her mistress when the slave conceived. Sarai responded in a way that seems to be an instance of personal pique:

And Sarai said to Abram, "May the wrong done to me be on you! I gave my maid to your embrace, and when she saw that she had conceived, she looked on me with contempt. May the LORD judge between you and me!" But Abram said to Sarai, "Behold, your maid is in your power; do to her as you please." Then Sarai dealt harshly with her, and she fled from her. (Gen. 16:5f.)

Had we only the Old Testament as a resource, we might surmise that the wrong alleged by Sarai was that her slave was expressing contempt for her barren mistress by claiming the child as her own. The Code of Hammurabi, however, contains a provision dealing with this situation:

> If a man has married a priestess and she has given a slave-girl
> to her husband and she bears sons, [if] thereafter that slave-
> girl goes about making herself equal to her mistress, be-
> cause she has borne sons, her mistress shall not sell her; she
> may put the mark [of a slave] on her and may count her with
> the slave-girls. If she has not borne sons, her mistress may
> sell her.[44]

Here, a slave girl remains the property of her mistress
even when she has been assigned to her owner's husband
as a concubine. A significant degree of relationship is
believed by scholars to have existed among various ancient Semitic legal traditions.[45] As a result, it is entirely
possible that an action reported in the Old Testament
may reflect a legal situation reported in the Code of
Hammurabi. Such seems to be the case here.[46]

If we are correct in thinking that the law quoted from
the Code of Hammurabi reports the legal background
for the story of Sarai and Hagar, matters become much
clearer. Hagar had acted as if her pregnancy had made
her a freewoman. Sarai asked Abram to confirm Hagar's
legal standing. Abram responded in terms of the ancient
Near Eastern legal tradition preserved for us now in the
Code of Hammurabi. Hagar, even though a concubine
and pregnant, remained Sarai's slave. She thus remained
subject to Sarai's authority.

We can conclude this section with a psalm in which the
dependence of the righteous upon God is likened to the
dependence of servant upon master and maidservant
upon mistress:

> Behold, as the eyes of servants
> look to the hand of their master,
> as the eyes of a maid
> to the hand of her mistress,
> so our eyes look to the LORD our God,
> till he have mercy upon us.
>   (Ps. 123:2)

V

The most unexpected chapter in the story of the relationships of husbands and wives in ancient Israel is the one that describes the wives as superior to their husbands.[47] In a few cases, wives appear to have been the social superiors of their husbands. The Egyptian Pharaoh is reported as having given his daughters in marriage to cement alliances to Solomon (I Kings 3:1) and Hadad of Damascus (I Kings 11:19f.). Solomon married two of his daughters to officials placed in charge of two of the administrative districts into which the kingdom had been divided (I Kings 4:11, 15). As princesses, these wives may have outranked their husbands. Ben Hadad's Egyptian wife bore him one son, who was reared in the court of the Pharaoh (I Kings 11:20), but we are given no information about the other marriages.

If there were parity between husband and wife, we should find instances in which the wife prevailed over the husband. Examples of this are rare in the Old Testament, and this seems to be significant until we remember that examples of the domination of a wife by her husband also are rare.

When Sarah became a mother and saw her son playing with the child of Hagar, Sarah's bondwoman, "she said to Abraham, 'Cast out this slave woman with her son; for the son of this slave woman shall not be heir with my son Isaac' " (Gen. 21:10). Even though Abraham did not want to comply, he did so. The Biblical narrative reports that God persuaded him to assent. The Babylonian law quoted earlier here, however, suggests that Sarah demanded and got her legal rights.

A more striking example is the story of Abigail and

Nabal in I Sam. 25:2–38. Nabal was a wealthy Carmelite of whom David asked a gift because his band had done Nabal no harm. Nabal refused, and David decided to give Nabal a demonstration of what he had been spared. Abigail, Nabal's wife, heard about the matter and gathered two hundred loaves of bread, two skins of wine, five dressed sheep, five measures of dried grain, one hundred clusters of raisins, and two hundred cakes of figs and sent them ahead by her own servants while she followed. When she and David met, she made peace with David. The raid was canceled. When Abigail returned home, she found her husband feasting and drunken. "And in the morning, when the wine had gone out of Nabal, his wife told him these things, and his heart died within him, and he became as a stone. And about ten days later the LORD smote Nabal; and he died." (I Sam. 25:37f.)

Jezebel is the wife whose domination of her husband receives the greatest attention in the Old Testament. She is reported to have slaughtered the prophets of her husband's god (I Kings 18:13) and to have maintained a staff of 850 professional servants of her god at court (v. 19). She is at her most vivid in the story of Naboth's vineyard. King Ahab wanted Naboth's vineyard for the palace vegetable garden, but Naboth refused to sell his family's inheritance. Thereupon Ahab "lay down on his bed, and turned away his face, and would eat no food."

> But Jezebel his wife came to him, and said to him, "Why is your spirit so vexed that you eat no food?" And he said to her, "Because I spoke to Naboth the Jezreelite, and said to him, 'Give me your vineyard for money; or else, if it please you, I will give you another vineyard for it'; and he answered, 'I will not give you my vineyard.' " And Jezebel his wife said to him, "Do you now govern Israel? Arise, and eat bread, and let your heart be cheerful; I will give you the vineyard of Naboth the Jezreelite!" (I Kings 21:5–7)

What is a wife to do when her husband won't play his part? Jezebel trumped up charges of blasphemy and treason against Naboth and had them pressed by false witnesses. When Naboth had been dealt with according to the deserts she had decreed for him, she advised her husband to seize the property, and he complied (I Kings 21:8–16).

There also are a few reports in the Old Testament of a wife giving her husband advice. The most detailed is the least historical, the angelic visitation to the wife of Manoah which announced to her that she would bear a son who was to be dedicated to the Lord. When the sequence of extraordinary events culminated with the angel ascending to heaven in the flame of the sacrifice offered up by the nervous couple,

> Manoah said to his wife, "We shall surely die, for we have seen God." But his wife said to him, "If the LORD had meant to kill us, he would not have accepted a burnt offering and a cereal offering at our hands, or shown us all these things, or now announced to us such things as these." (Judg. 13:22f.)

Did the conversation between husband and wife lend an air of reality to the legend because the conversation reflected a well-known marital relationship?

Two other fictional narratives also report the wife advising her husband. The first appears in the prose prologue and epilogue for the poem which makes up the bulk of The Book of Job. This has often been held by scholars originally to have existed independently from the poem because the style and content of the two differ so much. The prose narrative tells of the testing of a righteous man by Satan, an angel, to determine whether or not he will remain righteous under undeserved tribulation. Job first lost property, sons and daughters, then his health. In the midst of this calamity, his wife said to him, "Do you still hold fast your integrity? Curse God, and die." But he said to her, "You speak as one of the foolish women would speak. Shall we receive good at the hand of God, and shall we not receive evil?" In all this Job did not sin with his lips. (Job 2:9f.)

Three features of this story merit notice. The wife does not hesitate to advise her husband on one of the major problems of the Old Testament: are the righteous rewarded by God? Nor does her advice conform to the pious stereotype of a wife. And Job's reply avoids another stereotype, the picture of all women as foolish. The image conveyed is of a wife able and willing to advise her husband, and of a husband who respected his wife's advice and thus protested when she spoke foolishly.

In The Book of Esther, Zeresh, the wife of Haman, is described as advising her husband twice. It was she and his friends who suggested that Haman, infuriated because Mordecai refused to pay him the homage due him by royal edict, should build a gallows and advise the king to execute Mordecai on it (Esth. 5:13f.). When Haman received his first hint that he had been outmaneuvered by Esther, he went home.

And Haman told his wife Zeresh and all his friends everything that had befallen him. Then his wise men and his wife Zeresh said to him, "If Mordecai, before whom you have begun to fall, is of the Jewish people, you will not prevail against him but will surely fall before him." (Esth. 6:13)

Here, Zeresh is reported as acting in concert with the wise men who advised the man who advised the king.

All three of these narratives picturing a wife as advising her husband are fiction. The dates assigned them range from early to late. Thus the motif of the wise wife was a stable one in ancient Israelite culture. Furthermore, the theme plays different roles in these examples. In the first, the sagacity of the wife is the means by which the authenticity of the blessing given in the theophany is established. In the second, the recommendation of Job's wife is the statement of the commonsense response to Job's sufferings over against which he is enabled to affirm his faithfulness to God. In the third, the wise wife and friends play the role of the chorus in a Greek tragedy, underscoring or accentuating the thrust of the story. It therefore seems likely that the motif of the wise wife reflected a commonplace reality in ancient Israelite culture.

Finally, we have a series of examples of wives manipulating their husbands. This way of influencing a husband has been magnified wholly out of proportion. Johannes Pedersen's comment about it is typical of many:

> The will of the husband is the will of the house; the woman must often act by underhand means and use cunning in order to have her way. A typical example of this kind of woman's cunning is when Rebekah makes the blind father give Jacob his blessing.[48]

If Rebekah's deception of her husband is an example of "woman's cunning," then some of the men whose cunning is described in the Old Testament suffered from a sexual identity crisis! The list of such "feminine" males would include Abraham tricking the Pharaoh into believing Sarah to be Abraham's sister (Gen. 12:10–20 and the parallel narratives in chs. 20; 26:1–11), Jacob tricking Laban, his father-in-law, in order to build up his own flocks (Gen. 30:25–43), Saul's attempts to kill David (I Sam. 18:17–27), David's plot leading to the death of Uriah after less lethal tricks had failed (II Sam. 11:6–25), and the ruse used by Joab, the commander of David's army, to secure the return of Absalom to Jerusalem after that prince had ordered the killing of his brother (II Sam.

14:1–21). This list is incomplete, but it should be enough evidence to refute the contention that cunning was a female trait in ancient Israel. The evidence already presented here describing situations in which wives exerted influence or domination over their husbands by other means is also proof that cunning was not the only avenue (or even the chief one) open to the wife to influence her husband.

There are at least six examples in the Old Testament of women using cunning to gain their ends: Rebekah's deception of Isaac (Gen. 27:5 to 28:5), the Israelite midwives' evasion of the Pharaoh's commands (Ex. 1:15–19), Samson's defeat at the hands of his wife (Judg. 14:15–18) and his mistress (ch. 16:4–21), Bathsheba's manipulation of the senile David (I Kings 1:11–31), and Esther's campaign to remove Haman from her royal husband's favor (Esth. 5:1 to 7:10). Each of these is a lively tale, and only the fact that all illustrate the same point justifies selective reporting. Fortunately, nearly all of them are discussed in a different context elsewhere here, and we can report one only as representative of all of the group.

The Book of Esther opens when Ahasuerus, king of Persia, demotes Vashti, his queen, because she disobeyed him. After an extensive search, Esther, a Jewish maiden, becomes Vashti's successor; and Mordecai, her guardian, takes up his position near the gate of the palace in order to be able to advise his ward. In the meantime, Haman has been elevated to a position in the court second only to the king and uses his position to exact the homage he judges to be suitable to his new position. Mordecai, the Jew, refuses to grant it, and Haman's pique against Mordecai becomes a monstrous plot to exterminate all of Mordecai's race. The king trusts Haman's guidance and grants him the authority to carry out his plan. Royal couriers carry the necessary edicts throughout the empire.

When Mordecai learns of the plan, he advises Esther to act. She secures an audience with Ahasuerus and asks that she be permitted to have the king and Haman as dinner guests. Her petition is granted, and Haman jubilantly announces his most recent honor to his wife and friends. His triumph is marred only by the continued refusal of Mordecai to pay homage to him. He is advised to build a gallows and persuade the king to hang Mordecai on it. That same night, the king, unable to sleep, reviews the royal chronicles and reads there of Mordecai's help earlier in thwarting a plot against the throne. When Haman arrives to take up the day's duties, the king asks his advice on how to reward "the man whom the king delights to honor." Haman thinks himself to be that man and describes fulsomely what should be done. He is ordered to carry it out with Mordecai as its recipient. He returns home to seek consolation from his wife and friends just as the summons to Esther's dinner arrives.

The dinner swiftly becomes a catastrophe for Haman. The king is so pleased with the dinner that he asks Esther what further petition he may grant her. She asks that the sentence of death against her and her people be revoked, identifying Haman as the author of the plot:

> Then Haman was in terror before the king and the queen. And the king rose from the feast in wrath and went into the palace garden; but Haman stayed to beg his life from Queen Esther, for he saw that evil was determined against him by the king. And the king returned from the palace garden to the place where they were drinking wine, as Haman was falling on the couch where Esther was; and the king said, "Will he even assault the queen in my presence, in my own house?" As the words left the mouth of the king, they covered Haman's face. (Esth. 7:6b–8)

Haman is executed on the gallows he had caused to be raised for Mordecai; a new royal edict authorizes the Jews to avenge themselves on those who had sought their death; and Esther and Mordecai institute the Feast of Purim to honor the deliverance of their people. The wilier Esther had triumphed over the wily Haman.

VI

In this chapter we have reviewed the evidence which indicates that the ancient Israelite woman wielded power in the home at least equal to that exercised by the husband. Oddly enough, it is necessary to introduce a commonsense corrective in our summary of our findings in order to support the conclusion just stated. The position of the queen mother (and presumably its equivalent in a nonroyal family) was unique. A queen became queen mother only after her husband had died. Then the authority over children which husband and wife had once shared passed entirely to the mother.

In general, the picture that has emerged is strikingly modern. Husband and wife seem to have lived together in an essential parity within which differentiation of function based on sexual identity was present. The parity, however, was not so rigid that it made impossible the domination of the marriage by a stronger will or the deference of one to the other in areas of admitted superiority. The wise wife was far from unknown, just as a husband noted for his wisdom was also not unknown.

Marriage did not condemn the woman to a life of servitude. She did not lose control of slaves given her by her family, even when she assigned a slave to her husband as a concubine. She did not surrender the right to engage in business on her own (see Prov. 31:10–27), or to dispose of family goods. There is no evidence that she was sequestered, and the clear implication of several of the laws bearing on her conduct is that she moved freely throughout the community. She shared fully with her husband the responsibility over the children, exercising it alone when she became a widow; she played an active public role when queen mother; she had significant oversight of servants in the household; and she participated freely and as an equal in decisions involving the life of her husband or her family.

The naming of children has been taken by anthropologists to be one index of the division of authority within the family between husband and wife, with the right to name the child an exercise of authority. The act of naming a child is mentioned forty-seven times in the Old Testament. The mother named the child in twenty-four instances (Gen. 4:25, 19:37, 38; 29:32, 33, 34, 35; 30:6, 8, 11, 13, 18, 20, 21, 24; 35:18a; 38:4, 5; Judg. 13:24; I Sam. 1:20; 4:21; I Chron. 4:9; 7:16; Isa. 7:14), and the women of the village once (Ruth 4:17). Men named children sixteen times (Gen. 4:26; 5:3, 29; 16:15; 21:3; 35:18b; 41:51, 52; Ex. 2:22; II Sam. 12:24; I Chron. 7:23; Job 42:14 [3 daughters]; Gen. 25:25 [masc. pl.]). In four instances, prophets named their children as acted signs conveying the word of the Lord (Isa. 8:3; Hos. 1:4, 6, 9), raising the total in which men named a child to twenty. Once an angel instructed a woman to name a child (Gen. 16:11), and once God directed a man (Gen. 17:19). If the last two instances be eliminated, women name children twenty-five times and men twenty,[49] a ratio which reflects the description of the relationship of husband and wife being presented here far better than it does the traditional patriarchal picture of the Hebrew family.

CHAPTER 7

Sisters, Divorcées, Widows

I

Not every woman in the household was a wife or a daughter. In the story of Tamar, David's daughter, we have an example of an unmarried sister living with her brother (II Sam. 13:20). This suggests that a woman's relationships with her siblings were significant. We also have learned that parents could secure a divorce for daughters (Judg. 15:1f.; I Sam. 25:44). Apparently a divorced woman retained standing in the family into which she had been born. Finally, our references to The Book of Ruth and the discussion of the queen mother have raised the question of the widow. The evidence that describes each condition will be reviewed in this chapter.

II

The relationship between siblings often was very close. In the prose framework of the poem of Job, Job's seven sons invite one another and their three sisters to feasts in their homes (Job 1:4, 13, 18f.), and Job's brothers and sisters come to visit him after he has been restored to health and prosperity (ch. 42:11). In The Song of Solomon, the bond between brother and sister is a simile for the love of bride and groom (S. of Sol. 4:10–12; 8:1f.).

Sexual relations between siblings were sternly prohibited, in spite of the erotic overtones of the passages in The Song of Solomon. The oldest example is Deut. 27: 22: "Cursed be he who lies with his sister, whether the daughter of his father or the daughter of his mother." This was restated twice as a law (Lev. 18:9; 20:17) and extended to cover the relationship between a man and his maternal aunt (Lev. 20:19).

Two stories in the Old Testament report brothers avenging the rape of their sisters. The first of these, the rape of Dinah, the daughter of Jacob, by Shechem (Gen., ch. 34), probably is tribal history told as legend since Shechem was a prominent and ancient city-state in Palestine. The story now ends with the slaughter of the men of "the city," and the history behind the legend may have been an Israelite attack on the city of Shechem. The assault is carried out by Simeon and Levi, and Gen. 49: 5–7 also may report the incident.[50] The gist of the tale is that an unmarried woman is raped by a youth who then seeks to marry her. The condition set by the victim's family is the circumcision of all the males of the city. When they have complied,

> on the third day, when they [the men of the city] were sore, two of the sons of Jacob, Simeon and Levi, Dinah's brothers, took their swords and came upon the city unawares, and killed all the males. They slew Hamor and his son Shechem with the sword, and took Dinah out of Shechem's house and went away. (Vs. 25f.)

When Jacob reproached them for their deed, "they said, 'Should he treat our sister as a harlot?' " (v. 31).

It was the full brothers of Dinah, those sharing with her both father and mother, who avenged her; and it also was the full brother, Absalom, who avenged the rape of Tamar by her half brother (II Sam., ch. 13). In a polygamous family, at least in these two stories, the full brother gives the unmarried sister the fullest legal protection possible. This may reflect a legal obligation not reported in the law codes, or it may indicate that the bonds of affection between children of the same mother were particularly strong.

A similar closeness between siblings appears in laws describing a priest's cultic cleanness:

> And the LORD said to Moses, "Speak to the priests, the sons of Aaron, and say to them that none of them shall defile himself for the dead among his people, except for his nearest of kin, his mother, his father, his son, his daughter, his brother, or his virgin sister (who is near to him because she has no husband; for her he may defile himself)." (Lev. 21: 1–3; see also Ezek. 44:25)

Contact with a dead body so defiled a priest that he could not mediate between God and people; but the requirement of ritual purity yielded to the more primal demands of family defined as parents, children, brothers, and unmarried sisters. The relationship between brothers and sisters could not have been based on affection because it applied only to unmarried sisters.

III

We have already had a hint of the status of a divorced woman in the reports of fathers terminating daughters' marriages (Judg. 15:1f.; I Sam. 25:44). These passages indicate that divorce was as much a family matter as had been the marriage. The woman continued to share in a corporate identity, thus to have selfhood as a member of a family. The divorce was a reversion from the family within which she might bear children to the family in which she had been a child. Divorce often was a prelude to remarriage, as in both the instances cited here.

The acceptance of divorce by the authors of the Old Testament has received more attention than it deserves, perhaps because of the hostility of the writers of the New Testament to it (see Mark 10:1–12 and Matt. 19:3–9). Not much is said about divorce in the Old Testament. Few instances of it are reported; it is mentioned infrequently in the laws, it was condemned unreservedly once, and it was held in such low esteem that it was used as a simile for Israel's faithlessness to God.

Reports of divorce are rare. In Gen. 21:14 we are told that Abraham sent Hagar away. Although Hagar had become Abraham's concubine, she continued to be Sarah's slave, and this divorce reflected Sarah's right to dismiss one of her own servants. The report of the relationship between Moses and Zipporah in Ex. 18:2–7 is unclear. Moses is said in v. 2 to have "sent her away," a phrase that might be taken to suggest divorce. But the narrative continues: "One told Moses, 'Lo, your father-in-law Jethro is coming to you with your wife and her two sons with her.' " This suggests that Moses had not secured a divorce but rather had entrusted his family to his father-in-law for safekeeping while he undertook a hazardous task.

One report of a divorce in the Old Testament is given us in the form of a prophet acting out the word of the Lord. Hosea married Gomer, daughter of Diblaim, in response to divine command (Hos. 1:2f.). She bore three children. Each child's name was an aspect of the word of the Lord being proclaimed by the prophet (ch. 1:4–9). After the birth of the third child, Hosea divorced Gomer for infidelity, equating what he had done with the Lord's repudiation of Israel for its faithlessness to its deity (ch. 2:2–13). Finally, Hosea is commanded to love an unnamed faithless woman just as God loves a faithless people (ch. 3).

The interpretation of Hos., chs. 1 to 3, is difficult. The marriage may have disintegrated when Hosea found that Gomer was participating in the local fertility shrine's rites. This not only would have called the paternity of the children into question, it also would have disrupted the marriage of a husband who advocated a strict Yahwism and a wife who practiced either Baalism or a synthesis of Yahwism and Baalism. Hosea thus may have come to see his marriage with Gomer as paralleling the relationship between God and Israel. God would be as much in the right in making void a covenant with faithless Israel as Hosea was in the right in repudiating a marriage contract with an unfaithful Gomer.

The tragedy, however, seems to have closed on a note of hope. Hosea stood in the strict Yahwist tradition out of which the Deuteronomic school later was to come. The prohibition in Deut. 24:1–4 of remarriage after a wife had married a second husband may explain why Hosea purchased Gomer (if the unnamed woman in Hos. 3:1 be Gomer). Holding her as a slave wife is not explicitly prohibited in Deut. 24:1–4. The purchase of Gomer is explained as an act of love greater than the wrong which earlier had led to the divorce.[51]

This reconstruction of the events behind Hos., chs. 1 to 3, yields several conclusions. Hosea 2:2 gives Gomer's adultery as the cause of the divorce. The use of divorce as a simile for the breakdown of the covenant between God and Israel (to which we will refer later) indicates that a wife's adultery was a widely acknowledged justification for terminating marriage. Hosea's statement,

> She is not my wife,
> and I am not her husband
> (Hos. 2:2)

is sometimes described as the legal declaration of divorce,[52] although there is no evidence to support the conclusion outside this verse. Verse 4, "Upon her children also I will have no pity, because they are children of harlotry," may indicate that the children of a marriage dissolved because of the wife's infidelity could be repudiated by the husband.

There seems to have been sufficient similarity in Hosea's mind between the marriage bond and the covenant between God and Israel for the former to be an illustration of the latter. This will be amply confirmed from other passages later. It is easy to conclude from surveys of marriage in the Old Testament that its dissolution could be secured by the husband for almost any reason, however trivial.[53] It is difficult to see how this could be correct, however, if the covenant between husband and wife were held to be similar in any significant way to the covenant between God and Israel.

Finally, the only reason we are given for the reestablishment of Hosea's marriage is that he is to buy "a woman who is beloved of a paramour and is an adulteress; even as the LORD loves the people of Israel, though they turn to other gods and love cakes of raisins" (Hos. 3:1). Hosea, ch. 3, seems best understood as an extension of the parallel in Hos. 2:2–13 between the marriage and the covenant between God and people, and the motive for restoring the nation's covenant attributed to the Lord is thus to be extended to Hosea's reason for reestablishing the marriage. In both instances, the motive was love. If this seems too modern a reason, our concept of ancient Israelite marriage may be at fault. The second marriage was concubinage for Gomer. She became her husband's slave. Yet this was the means by which love between man and woman circumvented a law intended to discourage remarriage after divorce.

Ezra 10:2–44 reports a mass divorce. The setting is the establishment of a theocracy under Ezra, one feature of which was the repudiation of marriages with non-Israelite women. They are pictured in the Old Testament as a source of the intrusion of alien elements into Israel's worship (as in I Kings 11:1–8). When it was learned that many had married outside their faith, Shecaniah ben Jehiel recommended that all foreign wives be divorced (Ezra 10:1–5). Since it was raining heavily, it was decided to take a census at a more convenient time to identify those who had married alien women. When the task was done, all who had so acted were named. "All these had married foreign women, and they put them away with their children" (v. 44). This was one of the means by which post-exilic Jews sought to preserve their identity and uniqueness in the midst of an alien environment. Thus the event tells us little about the status of the ancient Israelite woman or of her later Jewish descendant.

The grounds for divorce in ancient Israel are unclear. Hosea's action against Gomer was taken because of her sexual faithlessness (Hos. 2:2). This reason is cited elsewhere in the prophetic literature when divorce initiated by the husband becomes a simile for the Lord's action against a faithless Israel (i.e., Jer. 3:6–10, 19f.; Ezek. 16: 1–63).[54] No instance of a wife repudiating a husband is reported. As we have seen, the wife's father could terminate a daughter's marriage. In the case of David and Michal, Saul may have acted when David became an outlaw (I Sam. 25:44).[55]

No legal prescriptions dealing with divorce in the abstract have survived. This is what we should expect. Case law, which makes up the bulk of the laws recorded in the

Old Testament, deals with specific instances. One such judicial decision, however, was stated in a way which seems at first to give the grounds for divorce:

> When a man takes a wife and marries her, if then she finds no favor in his eyes because he has found some indecency in her, and he writes her a bill of divorce and puts it in her hand and sends her out of his house, and she departs out of his house, and if she goes and becomes another man's wife, and the latter husband dislikes her and writes her a bill of divorce and puts it in her hand and sends her out of his house, or if the latter husband dies, who took her to be his wife, then her former husband, who sent her away, may not take her again to be his wife, after she has been defiled; for that is an abomination before the LORD, and you shall not bring guilt upon the land which the LORD your God gives you for an inheritance. (Deut. 24:1–4)

The statement that the husband has "found some indecency" in the wife, or that he "dislikes" her, has been taken either to justify divorce on virtually any grounds or as being too vague to be helpful to us. The latter position has been taken by both G. Ernest Wright and Gerhard von Rad. Wright observed that the law seems to permit divorce "only for good cause."[56] Gerhard von Rad wrote:

> The meaning of "indecent," "objectionable" (cf. 23:14) must have been clear in the time of Deuteronomy; otherwise the matter would certainly have been defined more exactly. By Jesus' time it was being debated in the rabbinical schools whether in such cases a lapse on the part of the woman is in mind or whether she possessed some repellent quality.[57]

It is best to leave the matter in these vague and admittedly unsatisfactory terms. To infer more is to read more into the passage than our knowledge justifies.

Even though no instance of a wife securing a divorce is reported in the Old Testament, the grounds for such an action can be deduced from Ex. 21:7–11. Only vs. 10f. need to be reported here:

> If he [the husband] takes another wife to himself, he shall not diminish her food, her clothing, or her marital rights. And if he does not do these three things for her, she shall go out for nothing, without payment of money.

This law describes the safeguards protecting an Israelite concubine. Among them is her right to divorce her husband and to gain her freedom without payment if the husband denies support and sexual access to her after taking a second wife. As Mace observed, "If this were true of a mere concubine, one would expect it to hold good *a fortiori* in the case of a wife, who would have her family to take her part."[58] Thus, contrary to the belief that the Israelite husband alone had the right to secure a divorce, the evidence indicates that both husband and wife had such a right. The grounds on which the husband might divorce a wife included her adultery but otherwise are vaguely defined. By contrast, the grounds for the wife's actions are precisely defined: nonsupport and the denial of sexual access. In effect, the wife could secure a divorce if her husband denied to her the means to be a mother and the wherewithal to support herself and her child.

New Testament opposition to divorce is foreshadowed in the Old Testament. The bulk of the legal prescriptions dealing with it limit it. One law prohibited remarriage after the wife had been wedded to a second husband (Deut. 24:1–4). To this must be added prohibitions of the divorce of a wife falsely accused of the premarital loss of her virginity (Deut. 22:13–19) and of a ravished, unbetrothed virgin (Deut. 22:28f.). The law requiring the freeing of a slave wife at the time of divorce also discouraged divorce by exacting a property loss (the freeing of a slave) on the owner-husband (Deut. 21:14).

All these limitations appear in the Deuteronomic Code. The use of divorce as a simile for the punishment of Israel by God appears also at this time (as in passages reported earlier here in which Jeremiah and Ezekiel liken Israel to an adulterous wife). Equating divorce with the horror of divine judgment in the collapse and defeat of the nation must have done little to commend it!

Malachi, writing in the century following the exile, opposed divorce as explicitly and as strongly as did the author of Mark 10:2–12:

> And this again you do. You cover the LORD's altar with tears, with weeping and groaning because he no longer regards the offering or accepts it with favor at your hand. You ask, "Why does he not?" Because the LORD was witness to the covenant between you and the wife of your youth, to whom you have been faithless, though she is your companion and your wife by covenant. Has not the one God made and sustained for us the spirit of life? And what does he desire? Godly offspring. So take heed to yourselves, and let none be faithless to the wife of his youth. "For I hate divorce, says the LORD the God of Israel, and covering one's garment with violence, says the LORD of hosts. So take heed to yourselves and do not be faithless." (Mal. 2:13–16)

These words are the maturation of implications present from the earliest sources. God is the source of the life that is given to a man and a woman covenanted together before the Lord. Any act that violates the covenant to which God has become a witness, and thus defiles the gift of life which God then confers, flouts the sovereignty and work of God. Divorce thus has become as grave an offense against the will of the Lord to create life as is oppression which destroys the life that has been created.

Three motifs emerge in a review of the evidence in the Old Testament dealing with divorce. The first is that both marriage and divorce are a family rather than an individual matter. The wife's family continued to be able to represent her rights, and she could return to it if repudiated by her husband. The second is that husband and wife may have been more nearly equal in their access to divorce than has been supposed. The grounds upon which the wife might secure divorce (and freedom, if she were a concubine) were more clearly stated than were the grounds upon which the husband might take action. Finally, the material on divorce provides us with a clear and strong statement of the purpose of marriage. Since marriage was to give God the opportunity to give new life, we can rightly infer a high standing for the woman in whose womb that new life came into being.

IV

The widow is another category in which the status of woman is disclosed. The word for widow in Biblical Hebrew is *'almanah.* It is a feminine noun derived from the verb *'lm,* "to bind," "to be silent" (in the intensive mode). The English word "widow" designates any woman who has not remarried after the death of her husband. Chayim Cohen, however, defines the *'almanah* as often being a "once-married woman who no longer had any means of financial support."[59] Even this definition may prove to be too broad in the light of the information given us in passages in the Old Testament in which a widow is described.

A childless woman who has not remarried after the death of her husband is called a widow in several Old Testament passages. In a few instances we are informed that she was able to return to her father's household. Tamar, the daughter-in-law of Judah, was told to "remain a widow in your father's house" until Judah's third son had become old enough to become her husband (Gen. 38:11); and a priest's bereaved and childless daughter could return home and share the sanctified food which only the priest and his family could eat (Lev. 22:13). This example is all the more important for being in a law code. Even though case law arose out of a single judicial decision solving a specific case, the decision became a law when the situation with which it dealt arose fairly often. Thereupon it became a description of a category of situation rather than an individual case.

In other statements about a widow, however, she often was a woman not only bereft of husband but also lacking the support of any other adult male. This had two consequences: she had to be self-supporting, and she had lost the normal means of recourse to legal process.

One of the legends told about Elijah reported him as commanded by God to stay with a widow in Zarephthah during a drought. When he arrived and asked for something to eat, "she said, 'As the LORD your God lives, I have nothing baked, only a handful of meal in a jar, and a little oil in a cruse; and now, I am gathering a couple of sticks, that I may go in and prepare it for myself and my son, that we may eat it, and die' " (I Kings 17:12). In a similar story told about Elisha, the widow is described as being forced to surrender her children to a creditor (II Kings 4:1). In both of these passages, the bereaved woman is described as responsible for the support of minor children and unable to provide it.

II Samuel 14:1–24 describes one of the means by which a courtier might influence a king. The king is David. The courtier is Joab, the commander in chief of David's armies. Absalom, the oldest living son of David, had been banished after he had ordered Amnon, an older half brother, killed because Amnon had raped Tamar, Absalom's sister (II Sam., ch. 13). When Joab saw that David was obsessed with the situation, he sought to nudge the king into action by having a woman present a fictional case to David for judgment. The woman begins,

"Alas, I am a widow; my husband is dead" (v. 5). She had two sons, one of whom killed the other in a quarrel. Her relatives now want to execute the remaining son in retribution for the killing of the brother. The woman then appeals to David because the death of the remaining son "would quench my coal which is left, and leave to my husband neither name nor remnant upon the face of the earth" (v. 7). In this instance, it seems proper to define the widow as a woman who has no recourse to judicial processes other than through appeal to the king, because the men who would normally defend her rights, the members of the extended family of which she was a part, are the ones who seek to execute her remaining son. Thus her sons' accusers are those who would normally be her defenders.

In the light of these passages, it may be no accident that none of the bereaved women in The Book of Ruth are designated as widows. Naomi, who had lost husband and sons, returns to her husband's village because she is represented as having some claim on his kinsmen; and Ruth, the daughter-in-law of Naomi's husband, becomes the agent through whom the claim is realized. Similarly, Bathsheba is not described as a widow after David's death, possibly because she had then become the immensely powerful queen mother.

The evidence thus seems to suggest that the derivation of *'almanah* from *'lm*, "to be silent," should be taken seriously. A widow was a silent one, a person often denied participation in the economic and legal life of the community because she lacked identification with a family. If this definition be correct, her plight was extremely serious. She had so little standing in the community that she was regularly grouped with the resident alien, the person who was present physically but did not belong to the group (as in Deut. 14:29; Ps. 94:6; etc.). In a society in which selfhood was defined corporately, she had lost selfhood.

Confirmation for this interpretation appears in two kinds of passages: those dealing with the legal status of widows, orphans, and aliens, and those in which an Israel cut off from its God is likened to a widow.

Exodus 22:21–24 is typical of the first group of passages:

> You shall not wrong a stranger or oppress him, for you were strangers in the land of Egypt. You shall not afflict any widow or orphan. If you do afflict them, and they cry out to me, I will surely hear their cry; and my wrath will burn, and I will kill you with the sword, and your wives shall become widows and your children fatherless.

Since the Old Testament describes the Israelites when in Egypt as slaves (as in Ex. 5:15f.; Deut. 5:15; etc.), we can easily deduce the true standing of the sojourner, widow, and orphan.

The widow sometimes played a prominent and grim role in oracles in which Israel is described as under a judgment caused by its alienation from God:

You have rejected me, says the LORD,
   you keep going backward;
so I have stretched out my hand against you and destroyed
   you;—
I am weary of relenting.
I have winnowed them with a winnowing fork
   in the gates of the land;
I have bereaved them, I have destroyed my people;
   they did not turn from their ways.
I have made their widows more in number
   than the sand of the seas;
I have brought against the mothers of young men
   a destroyer at noonday;

> I have made anguish and terror
> fall upon them suddenly.
>   (Jer. 15:6–8; see also ch. 18:21; Lam. 5:1–3)

Jeremiah turned here to the plight of the widow when seeking a simile to convey the enormity of the disaster that divine judgment would bring.

Even though the widow seems to have had no status in ancient Israel, she does have status in the Old Testament. The ancient Israelite definition of selfhood and its organization of society had no place for the resident alien, widow, or orphan. The Old Testament, a literature emerging out of the life of a community of faith, explicitly and repeatedly places the welfare of these three groups of outcasts under the care of God. We have already noted Ex. 22:21–24 and Deut. 27:19, verses in which this is stated. Deut. 10:17f. is another such passage:

> For the LORD your God is God of gods, and LORD of lords, the great, the mighty, and the terrible God, who is not partial and takes no bribe. He executes justice for the fatherless and the widow, and loves the sojourner, giving him food and clothing.

Giving the widow identity and status under God is not a platitude in the Old Testament. The passage just quoted continues: "Love the sojourner therefore; for you were sojourners in the land of Egypt" (v. 19). Although the authors of the Old Testament were consistent and clear in their assertions that the Lord gave the widow what society denied her, they also stated repeatedly that the faithful Israelite was commanded by God to protect the widow. This is stated both negatively and positively.

Stated negatively, the Lord's concern for the widow not only yielded the curse on the person "who perverts the justice due to the sojourner, the fatherless, and the widow" (Deut. 27:19), it was expressed also in a series of prophetic oracles of woe. This is familiar to us in passages in the major prophets such as Isa. 10:1f. and Ezek. 22:6f. But it also was a motif in lesser-known, post-exilic prophets:

> Then I will draw near to you for judgment; I will be a swift witness against the sorcerers, against the adulterers, against those who swear falsely, against those who oppress the hireling in his wages, the widow and the orphan, against those who thrust aside the sojourner, and do not fear me, says the LORD of hosts. (Mal. 3:5)

These passages report a continuous and consistent tradition covering a period of from approximately 740 to 450 B.C. in which prophetic mediators between God and people transmitted as a word from the Lord a condemnation of the people for their exploitation of the sojourner, orphan, and widow. These are not isolated statements, and their theme appears as often in positive injunctions as in condemnations. Thus Jeremiah was entrusted with a word of restoration should the people cleanse their lives:

> For if you truly amend your ways and your doings, if you truly execute justice one with another, if you do not oppress the alien, the fatherless or the widow, or shed innocent blood in this place, and if you do not go after other gods to your own hurt, then I will let you dwell in this place, in the land that I gave of old to your fathers for ever. (Jer. 7:5–7)

Isaiah earlier (Isa. 1:17) and Zechariah later (Zech. 7:9f.) joined with Jeremiah in this "word from the LORD."

This is highly specific. This word of the Lord exhorted the righteous to take upon themselves the responsibility for becoming the legal voice for the "silent ones," to take their part in a court of law just as a close kinsman would have done had there been one. The Deuteronomic legislators became even more explicit in describing a specific kind of injustice: "You shall not pervert the justice due to the sojourner or to the fatherless, or take a widow's garment in pledge" (Deut. 24:17). From this law we gain an unwelcome insight into the grimness of the extremity a widow deprived of family support might face. These same legislators also stated the right of the defenseless to glean a once-harvested crop:

> When you reap your harvest in your field, and have forgotten a sheaf in the field, you shall not go back to get it; it shall be for the sojourner, the fatherless, and the widow; that the LORD your God may bless you in all the work of your hands. When you beat your olive trees, you shall not go over the boughs again; it shall be for the sojourner, the fatherless, and the widow. When you gather the grapes of your vineyard, you shall not glean it afterward; it shall be for the sojourner, the fatherless, and the widow. You shall remember that you were a slave in the land of Egypt; therefore I command you to do this. (Deut. 24:19–22)

Ruth and Naomi seem to have used this right to call their plight to the attention of distant relatives after they had returned to Naomi's village (Ruth 2:1f., 18).

Finally, the care of the Lord for those lacking the support of a family was expressed in the law governing the use of the tithe:

> At the end of every three years you shall bring forth all the tithe of your produce in the same year, and lay it up within your towns; and the Levite, because he has no portion or inheritance with you, and the sojourner, the fatherless, and the widow, who are within your towns, shall come and eat and be filled; that the LORD your God may bless you in all the work of your hands that you do. (Deut. 14:28f.; see ch. 26:12–15)

The magnitude of God's care for widows is revealed nowhere more clearly than here. The Levites were a landless tribe which had become professional servants of the

Lord. Their livelihood came to them through their share
of tithes and sacrifices given to God by the faithful. Yet
they were here required to share their access to gifts
given God with widows, orphans, and sojourners.

We have already indicated that the three groups often
named together—the resident alien, the widow, and the
orphan—were in the same situation in the community.
All three lacked participation in an Israelite family that
could provide economic and legal security. These three
groups represented, in Israelite antiquity, the dispos-
sessed in much the same way that a refugee without resources does today. Desperate though the plight of the
widow must have been to have been grouped with the
sojourner and orphan, her presence there provides two
insights into her status.

The first is to be deduced from the obvious fact that
sojourners and orphans would include both females and
males. The trilogy of sojourner, widow, and orphan were
equal in their misfortunes regardless of their sex. A male
sojourner had no advantage over the Israelite widow
without family. As we have seen before in this study, an
equality of the sexes emerges far more often in a careful
study of the status of woman in the Old Testament than
we had been led to expect.

But that same equality between the sexes is present in
the consistent, centuries-long proclamation of the word
of the Lord. The God of Israel is the self-proclaimed
kinsman of both the male sojourner and the widow. It
was circumstance that mattered, not gender.

It would hardly be an exaggeration to say that the
widow represents the gravest extremity in which the ancient Israelite woman might find herself. The derivation
of the word for "widow," *'almanah,* suggests that a widow
was likely to be a woman who found herself deprived of
family identity through the death of her mate. She was
less than a person because she had been deprived of the

context (a family) in which selfhood was known. She occupies this tragic place along with orphans, male and female, for whom no family provided identity, and the resident alien whose family lived in another land.

Yet she had status even in extremity. At the very least, she was equal to all others, male and female, in a like situation. Far more to the point, however, she was of such importance to the God who had created Israel to be a people of the Lord that God became her next of kin in order to provide security for her through the actions of those among the people who heeded God's will. Her lot was desperate, but her standing was as high as that of the Levites, the servants of God.

V

This chapter has reviewed materials essential for any well-rounded picture of woman in ancient Israelite society. The information provided us confirms essentially the estimate of the status of woman deduced from a review of their place as daughters and wives with a single, but significant, exception: the standing of the widow in the community of the faithful as one whose kinsman was God. The role of the *go'el*, the kinsman charged with defending the rights of another, was so important and elevated in ancient Israel that the Second Isaiah described the Lord as Israel's *go'el*, during the bleak years of the exile (Isa. 41:14; 43:14; 44:6; etc.), knowing that his words would give his people a sense of their worth. For centuries, the prophets of the Old Testament proclaimed the Lord to be the *go'el* of the sojourner, the widow, and the orphan.

CHAPTER 8

Freedom of Action

I

Since the family was the basic unit of ancient Israelite society, it is not surprising that much of the Old Testament material which we can use to reconstruct the status of woman describes her role and standing in the family. A study of the position of the male also would have to begin with his place in the family. Larger social structures —village, tribe, and nation—did exist, however, and we need now to review evidence indicating how women functioned in these areas. We will examine the woman's freedom of movement, her involvement in public affairs, her role in the economy, and her participation in the cult. This chapter will deal with the first three of these. The next chapter will examine woman's role in the cult.

II

The most elementary criterion for determining participation in society outside the home is freedom of movement. Wives confined to the home are automatically excluded from much of the life of the community.

When we seek to describe this facet of the life of an ancient Israelite woman, we are influenced far too much by Arab seclusion of women.[60] We find our preconceptions confirmed by the picture we seem to be given of Sarah eavesdropping on the conversation of Abraham with his guests from her seclusion in her tent (Gen. 18:9). If, however, we let the Scriptures speak for themselves, a quite different picture emerges.

A series of passages which are to be dated over a period of several centuries picture girls and women as moving quite freely outside the home. The Yahwist source in the Pentateuch twice reports unmarried daughters as coming alone to a well to draw water for their father's flocks. Both stories give the setting in which a future wife is met. One relates:

> Now the priest of Midian had seven daughters; and they came and drew water, and filled the troughs to water their father's flock. The shepherds came and drove them away; but Moses stood up and helped them, and watered their flock. When they came to their father Reuel, he said, "How is it that you have come so soon today?" They said, "An Egyptian delivered us out of the hand of the shepherds, and even drew water for us and watered the flock." He said to his daughters, "And where is he? Why have you left the man? Call him, that he may eat bread." (Ex. 2:16b–20; see also Gen. 29:4–14)

Watering the father's flock seems to have been the girls' responsibility. They also seem regularly to have been driven away from the watering troughs by shepherds tending other flocks. Thus these unmarried girls carried a family responsibility outside the home which exposed them to the superior force of a group of shepherds. Both here and in Gen. 29:4–14 the girl is apparently expected to invite a helpful stranger into the home.

The report of the visit of the Queen of Sheba to the court of Solomon (I Kings 10:1-13 = II Chron. 9:1-12) cannot be used as a portrayal of Israelite custom during the monarchy. She was not an Israelite. However, the laws in Deuteronomy dealing with rape also come from the period of the monarchy, even though they are later than the time of Solomon. Deuteronomy 22:25 prescribes, "But if in the open country a man meets a young woman who is betrothed, and the man seizes her and lies with her, then only the man who lay with her shall die." This passage presupposes the freedom of a young woman to move about alone in the open country. This law is known as "case law." It arose out of a specific case and was preserved because the situation it described happened often enough to make the recording of a decision about it useful.

The "Isaianic Apocalypse" in Isa., chs. 24 to 27, often is dated by scholars between 550 and 450 B.C., and it thus comes from the age after the time of the monarchy. It provides still another witness to the freedom of ancient Israelite women to move about outside the village by describing them as gathering firewood in the wilderness (ch. 27:11).

The passages cited represent a span of time from at least the ninth to fifth centuries B.C., and they contain a variety of kinds of literature. The two from the Yahwist stratum are from sagas and reflect either folk custom at the time they were composed or the popular view then of life in former times. The law from Deuteronomy is case law, emerging out of a concrete instance and preserved because the situation arose often. An oracle of woe from a post-exilic apocalypse also was cited. In the light of the long span of time covered and the variety of literary types represented, we are justified in concluding that women in ancient Israel were free to move about outside the home, not only within the village but also in

the open country. The freedom to move in the community at large creates the possibility of access to activities
outside the home.

III

Women are reported as discharging various activities
in ancient Israel which we associate only with the male:
leading the community in peace and war, usurping the
throne, building a city, and engaging in combat.

Three narratives report women as leading their community in peace and war. The oldest is Judg., ch. 5, an
ancient epic poem telling of an Israelite victory over the
Canaanites. Deborah and Barak were the Israelite lead-
ers. Deborah's role is described twice in the poem:

> The peasantry ceased in Israel, they ceased
>   until you arose, Deborah,
>   arose as a mother in Israel.
>
> (V. 7)
>
> Awake, awake, Deborah!
>   Awake, awake, utter a song!
>   Arise, Barak, lead away your captives,
>   O son of Abinoam.
>
> (V. 12)

A third allusion to Deborah appears in the roster of the
tribes:

> The princes of Issachar came with Deborah,
>   and Issachar faithful to Barak;
>   into the valley they rushed forth at his heels.
>
> (V. 15a)

Deborah is pictured in these lines as having aroused the
Israelite tribesmen and having sustained their fighting
zeal. Barak appears to have been the military leader. The
relationship between Deborah and Barak is reported in

greater detail in the later prose version of the same campaign (Judg., ch. 4, esp. vs. 6 to 8).

A woman provided crucial leadership in the suppres-
sion of Sheba's revolt against David:

> And Sheba passed through all the tribes of Israel to Abel of
> Beth-maacah; and all the Bichrites assembled, and followed
> him in. And all the men who were with Joab came and
> besieged him in Abel of Beth-maacah; they cast up a mound
> against the city, and it stood against the rampart; and they
> were battering the wall, to throw it down. Then a wise
> woman called from the city, "Hear! Hear! Tell Joab, 'Come
> here, that I may speak to you.' " And he came near her; and
> the woman said, "Are you Joab?" He answered, "I am."
> Then she said to him, "Listen to the words of your maidserv-
> ant." And he answered, "I am listening." Then she said,
> "They were wont to say in old time, 'Let them but ask coun-
> sel at Abel'; and so they settled a matter. I am one of those
> who are peaceable and faithful in Israel; you seek to destroy
> a city which is a mother in Israel; why will you swallow up
> the heritage of the LORD?" Joab answered, "Far be it from
> me, far be it, that I should swallow up or destroy! That is not
> true. But a man of the hill country of Ephraim, called Sheba
> the son of Bichri, has lifted up his hand against King David;
> give up him alone, and I will withdraw from the city." And
> the woman said to Joab, "Behold, his head shall be thrown
> to you over the wall." Then the woman went to all the
> people in her wisdom. And they cut off the head of Sheba
> the son of Bichri, and threw it out to Joab. So he blew the
> trumpet, and they dispersed from the city, every man to his
> home. And Joab returned to Jerusalem to the king. (II Sam.
> 20:14–22)

Several details in this passage are interesting. The first
is the ability of the woman living in a besieged city to
summon the commander of the besieging army for a
parley. This hardly conveys the impression that she was
held to be an inferior either by Joab or by the narrator
of the story. The second is her readiness to commit her

city to a dangerous course of action. Her promise to have Sheba beheaded could not be kept unless the Bichrites, members of his clan and his supporters, were first disarmed. She is described as having gone "to all the people in her wisdom." We are given the impression of a woman gaining assent to her proposal because of widespread response to her sagacity. It hardly needs to be added that she could not have done what she did had she been confined to her home.

Lemuel, king of Massa, was taught proverbial wisdom by his mother (Prov. 31:1). The book of The Proverbs elsewhere links father and mother in the instruction of a child (e.g., 1:8f.; 6:20). The picture of the Babylonian queen advising her husband in Dan. 5:10–12 conforms in several of its features to the story of the wise woman of Beth-maacah. The Book of Daniel is judged by scholars to be a description of the crisis in 168 B.C. during the Seleucid rule in Jerusalem, even though it is written as a narrative laid in the earlier Babylonian era. It thus would be better to see it as describing a Jewish author's understanding of the role of woman in 168 B.C. than as an accurate description of the place of a Babylonian queen.

Descriptions of the activities of wise women are few in the Old Testament. However, the stories describe "a wise woman," not "the wise woman." The absence of the definite article (the equivalent in Hebrew to our indefinite article) attests to the presence of an undefined number of women whose wisdom was prized. It was simply "a wise woman of Tekoa" (II Sam. 14:2), or of Abel of Beth-maacah, not "the [only] wise woman of Tekoa."

The two narratives in the Old Testament telling of political action by women involve queens. This is not surprising since both incidents occurred during the monarchy. The first is Jezebel's subversion of the judicial process in order to secure a plot of ground for her husband. The second is the usurpation of the throne of

David by a queen mother who may have been Jezebel's daughter.

Elijah's contest with the 850 prophets of Baal and Asherah in Jezebel's entourage (I Kings 17:1 to 19:18) is reported as a struggle which had political significance. Its culmination was the destruction of Ahab's dynasty (I Kings 19:15–17)! The political character of Jezebel's activities, however, is clearer to our eyes in the story of Naboth's vineyard, a narrative discussed earlier here as an example of the domination of a husband by his wife. When Naboth refused to sell land Ahab wanted for a garden, Ahab sulkily accepted the decision. Jezebel, however, bribed two rascals to charge Naboth falsely with treason and blasphemy. When he had been convicted and executed, she told Ahab to take possession of the land (I Kings 21:1–16).

This incident is reported as an instance of royal oppression arousing divine anger. According to ancient Israelite belief, the land, which belonged to the Lord, had been given to the families which held the usufruct of it. Only the exhaustion of the family line through poverty or death extinguished the usufruct. Thus Naboth's determination to retain possession of his family's inheritance was a solemn religious duty. God also guaranteed justice in the courts, as the many prophetic injunctions on the matter attest (Amos 5:15; Isa. 10:1f.; etc.), and Jezebel's perversion of the judicial system was a violation both of orderly legal process and of the divine sanction given it. She justified her action to Ahab with the query, "Do you now govern Israel?" The clear implication was that he did so only formally, and that she would show him how to make form become reality. Thus another dimension of the narrative is a clash of royal ideologies. Naboth and Ahab were acting within a concept of monarchy in accordance with which the king was as much subject to the laws and to the sovereignty of the Lord as was the commoner. Jezebel acted within an understanding of the nature of the kingship in which the will of the king took precedence over law. She was the daughter of the king of Sidon (I Kings 16:31), the name given to both Tyre and Sidon at this time, and Ezekiel reports that the king of Tyre thought himself to be divine (Ezek. 28:1–10). Jezebel probably believed that the king was divine and that his will was the will of a god. Thus an incident that appears in the Old Testament as an act of royal oppression was also a political intervention. Jezebel acted on Ahab's behalf as she believed a king should act. It was a partial usurpation of the throne dictated by an understanding of the monarchy alien to Israel.[61]

The second report of a woman engaged in political activity at the highest level is the account of Athaliah's seizure of the throne in Jerusalem in II Kings 11:1–3. This has already been discussed in our review of the status of the queen mother. The conclusions reached there need only be repeated here. Athaliah, a daughter of Ahab, king of Israel, and wife of Jehoram, king of Judah, was the mother of Ahaziah, king of Judah. When Ahaziah, who was visiting Joram, king of Israel, at the time, was killed during a revolt against Joram (II Kings 9:22–28), Athaliah seized the throne in Jerusalem and tried to kill all Davidic claimants to it. She carried out her coup at the same time that Jehu was wiping out Athaliah's own family in the course of his revolution in the Northern Kingdom. Thus it is difficult to picture Athaliah as a figurehead for a revolt in Jerusalem inspired by the new ruler of the Northern Kingdom.

All things considered, it remains simplest and most probable to acknowledge that Athaliah acted primarily on her own, and that she was able to command sufficient power to remain on the throne for six years. The Chronicler, writing long after the event and using the report in II Kings 9:22–28 as his source, explained the incident:

"And the house of Ahaziah had no one able to rule the kingdom" (II Chron. 22:9b). As has been pointed out here earlier, the magnitude of Athaliah's achievement is to be measured by the fact that she was the only one in four centuries to succeed in the attempt to usurp the throne of David. Furthermore, Athaliah was the only woman to occupy the throne either in Jerusalem or Samaria (the capital of the Northern Kingdom).

A verse in one of the oracles of woe in the prophecies of Isaiah seems to imply a widespread belief that rule by a woman was equivalent to social decay:

> My people—children are their oppressors,
>   and women rule over them.
> O my people, your leaders mislead you,
>   and confuse the course of your paths.
>   (Isa. 3:12)

This verse cannot have been an allusion to the reign of Athaliah. Isaiah's ministry fell between 740 and 700 B.C. Athaliah ruled from 842 to 837 B.C., and Isaiah is unlikely to have described her reign as going on as he spoke. A close reading of the oracle suggests that Isaiah was predicting chaos when a child still governed by its mother occupied the throne. It was the immaturity of the child-king that was the affliction. Thus Isa. 3:12 hardly reflects a distrust of the capacity of a woman to rule in her own right.

The strangest chapter in a description of the participation of women in the public affairs of ancient Israel must surely be the one reporting women in military action. Three female warriors are mentioned. One was Deborah (Judg. 4:4–10; 5:1, 12–18), whose role has already been discussed. A second woman took an even more direct part in the conflict after the battle had ended. The commander of the defeated Canaanite army was Sisera. During flight following defeat, he took refuge temporarily with Heber, a Kenite. While he was resting, Jael, Heber's wife,

> put her hand to the tent peg
> and her right hand to the workmen's mallet;
> she struck Sisera a blow,
> she crushed his head,
> she shattered and pierced his temple.
> He sank, he fell,
> he lay still at her feet;
> at her feet he sank, he fell;
> where he sank, there he fell dead.
>   (Judg. 5:26f.; see also ch. 4:17–22)

The Book of Judges reports another woman using a different kind of nonmilitary hardwear with lethal results. Abimelech, the son of Gideon (or Jerubbaal) and a concubine, had been elected "king" of Shechem. Three years later, Gaal the son of Ebed persuaded the Shechemites to turn away from Abimelech (Judg. 9:1–4, 26–29). Abimelech responded by destroying the city. He then besieged Thebez, which also had participated in the revolt, broached its walls, and drove its defenders back into a heavily fortified tower. During his assault on the tower, "a certain woman threw an upper millstone upon Abimelech's head, and crushed his skull. Then he called hastily to the young man his armor-bearer, and said to him, 'Draw your sword and kill me, lest men say of me, "A woman killed him."' And his young man thrust him through, and he died" (Judg. 9:53f.). As has always been the case when professional military skills were being used against civilians, the civilians have had to respond with whatever was at hand. In this instance, military hardwear was no match for domestic hardwear.

Abimelech's fear of being known as a warrior whom a woman had killed proved to be justified. The incident was recalled centuries later by Joab, David's commander in chief (II Sam. 11:20f.). It is impossible now to determine whether the offense in Abimelech's death was that the act was done by a woman or by a civilian who happened to be a woman. Joab seems to have viewed it as a case of poor professional judgment. We can view Judg. 9:50–53 and II Sam. 11:20f. in a somewhat broader perspective. We may conclude from these passages that women participated in communal defense when such defense was a common responsibility.

The last reports of the involvement of women in public affairs are enigmatic. Nehemiah 3:12 describes the rebuilding of the walls of Jerusalem by various families under the direction of Nehemiah. One of those named is Shallum, whose daughters worked alongside him. The second is a genealogical notation:

> And Ephraim went in to his wife, and she conceived and bore a son; and he called his name Beriah, because evil had befallen his house. His daughter was Sheerah, who built both Lower and Upper Beth-horon, and Uzzen-sheerah. (I Chron. 7:23f.)

One daughter built three villages (or cities). Other daughters helped their father rebuild a part of the wall of Jerusalem. Both notations are preserved without comment. We do not know whether the actions attributed to these women were exceptional or unexceptional.

One thing is clear. Even though men obviously dominated the public sphere in ancient Israel, that realm was not closed to women. It has been said that "instances such as these prove nothing more than that strong personalities will assert themselves, wherever they are to be found, regardless of the existing order."[62] Were this the correct assessment of the evidence, we should find the "existing order" expressing itself in a fairly consistent condemnation of the yeasty females who had violated it. Such condemnation is absent (with the possible exception of Judg. 9:54). Therefore it would seem better to conclude that participation in public life was open to women. The relative scarcity of reports of their availing themselves of the possibility would better be attributed to their preoccupation with their more primary role in the family and its heavy demands upon them.

IV

Ancient Israel was not an industrial nation, and there seems to have been little separation between life in the family and participation in the economy. Nonetheless, the kinds of relationships that would be characteristic of family life and of economic life would have differed enough for it to have been possible for a woman to participate in the one without sharing in the other. Everyone shares in economic life simply as a consumer. Every woman ate food, wore clothing, used household utensils, and, often, added adornment of one kind or another to her basic wardrobe (see Isa. 3:18–23!). But did women hold property, sell goods, and buy land? If they are reported as doing these things, then they were economic persons in their own right.

The information available to us is obscured by the reality of corporate identity, exemplified by the primacy of the family, in ancient Israelite thought. An adult male normally was identified as the epitome of the family's identity, just as the king was the epitome of the nation's identity; and the family property at times is described as having belonged to that male. There are enough instances in which a woman had become the epitome of a family unit and had property rights focused on her, however, to justify two conclusions. The first is that property belonged to a family rather than to an individual. The second is that both men and women could be the epitome of a family and thus could appear to be "owning" property. Since all the evidence available reports the same situation, it will be reviewed here in the order of its appearance in the canon. The span of time covered by the materials is hard to establish because of the problem of dating some of the passages themselves, but it appears to be great.

The first example of women holding property rights is the inheritance of Zelophehad. He is described as "the son of Hepher, son of Gilead, son of Machir, son of Manasseh, from the families of Manasseh the son of Joseph" (Num. 27:1). He had died during the wilderness wanderings, leaving five daughters and no sons. The daughters petitioned Moses to be given their father's share of land in Canaan since his name, or his line of descent, would die out for lack of an inheritance:

> Moses brought their case before the LORD. And the LORD said to Moses, "The daughters of Zelophehad are right; you shall give them possession of an inheritance among their father's brethren and cause the inheritance of their father to pass to them. And you shall say to the people of Israel, 'If a man dies, and has no son, then you shall cause his inheritance to pass to his daughter.' " (Num. 27:5-8)

The heads of the other families of the tribe of Manasseh reopened the decision later, observing, "But if they are married to any of the sons of the other tribes of the people of Israel then their inheritance will be taken from the inheritance of our fathers, and added to the inheritance of the tribe to which they belong; so it will be taken away from the lot of our inheritance" (Num. 36:3). Thereupon Moses received a second word from the Lord: "Let them marry whom they think best; only, they shall marry within the family of the tribe of their father. The inheritance of the people of Israel shall not be transferred from one tribe to another; for every one of the people of Israel shall cleave to the inheritance of the tribe of his fathers" (vs. 6f.). Joshua 17:3-6 then reports the assigning of an inheritance to the daughters of Zelophehad.

Numbers, chs. 27 and 36, are post-exilic (i.e., come from 500 B.C. or later) in their present form. Thus the laws described here represent a matured legal tradition. The situation is clear. Land belonged to a family and to the tribe of which the family was a part. When a male could not act as the epitome of the family holding the property, a female acted. In neither case did the land belong to the individual acting as the epitome. The land always belonged to the group of which the individual was the representative. As was said earlier, there was a differentiation of function between the sexes within the family. The female, of biological necessity, bore the primary responsibility for the physical survival of the family through bearing children. The male, having a less demanding biological role, carried the responsibility of being the epitome of the family. When a male was lacking, however, a female took over that role also.

Other examples of women holding property include Rahab, the resident of Jericho who sheltered Joshua's spies (Josh. 2:1-15), the mother of Micah, an Ephraimite plundered by migrating Danites (Judg. 17:1ff.), Naomi (Ruth 4:1-6), and Job's daughters (Job 42:13-15). Rahab owned a house, Micah's mother "eleven hundred pieces of silver," Naomi a plot of land, and Job's daughters a share of their brother's inheritance. In each of these cases, there was an adult male in the family.

The material we have surveyed seems to point toward two related conclusions. The ownership of land appears to have been vested in the family, and its continued possession was essential to the survival of the family. The individual responsible for the family's property in a given generation was the family's epitome. Normally this was an adult male. Lacking an adult male, the epitome could be a female. Personal property, which seems to have included a house, household goods, precious metals, and probably clothing, could belong to an individual (female or male). This kind of property could be inherited by a daughter as well as by a son.

Did women engage in production and trade? At least two passages in the Old Testament indicate that they could, even though we might at first sight find it difficult to see what is being reported in the first as economic activity.

The first is the instruction from the Lord given Israelite women immediately before the flight from Egypt:

> And I will give this people favor in the sight of the Egyptians; and when you go, you shall not go empty, but each woman shall ask of her neighbor, and of her who sojourns in her house, jewelry of silver and of gold, and clothing, and you shall put them on your sons and on your daughters; thus you shall despoil the Egyptians. (Ex. 3:21f.)

Exodus 11:2 repeats the instruction, addressing it both to men and to women. Seeking booty is not an economic activity normally found in textbooks on economics, but it continues to be one of the ways in which property is transferred from one owner to another!

Proverbs 31:10–31 gives us the most complete example of economic activity reported in the Old Testament:

> A good wife who can find?
>   She is far more precious than jewels.
> The heart of her husband trusts in her,
>   and he will have no lack of gain.
> She does him good, and not harm,
>   all the days of her life.
> She seeks wool and flax,
>   and works with willing hands.
> She is like the ships of the merchant,

she brings her food from afar.
She rises while it is yet night
   and provides food for her household
   and tasks for her maidens.
She considers a field and buys it;
   with the fruit of her hands she plants a vineyard.
She girds her loins with strength
   and makes her arms strong.
She perceives that her merchandise is profitable.
   Her lamp does not go out at night.
She puts her hands to the distaff,
   and her hands hold the spindle.
She opens her hand to the poor,
   and reaches out her hands to the needy.
She is not afraid of snow for her household,
   for all her household are clothed in scarlet.
She makes herself coverings;
   her clothing is fine linen and purple.
Her husband is known in the gates,
   when he sits among the elders of the land.
She makes linen garments and sells them;
   she delivers girdles to the merchant.
Strength and dignity are her clothing,
   and she laughs at the time to come.
She opens her mouth with wisdom,
   and the teaching of kindness is on her tongue.
She looks well to the ways of her household,
   and does not eat the bread of idleness.
Her children rise up and call her blessed;
   her husband also, and he praises her:
"Many women have done excellently,
   but you surpass them all."
Charm is deceitful, and beauty is vain,
   but a woman who fears the LORD is to be praised.
Give her of the fruit of her hands,
   and let her works praise her in the gates.

This passage is a description of a wife given from the husband's point of view. It is stated several times that she lives within the family. Nonetheless, she acts on her own initiative in the economic world. She finds her wool and flax, she examines a field and buys it with money she has earned, "she perceives that her merchandise is profitable," and spins and weaves, selling the linen garments she makes. On one point, however, the passage is unclear. Does she keep the money she earns? Her husband is said to "have no lack of gain," but *The New English Bible* translates the phrase as "and children are not lacking." This much is clear: she does "provide food for her household," and its members are well dressed because of her labors.

V

Some evidence exists indicating that women had contacts with the royal court other than those available to them as daughters and wives. The evidence is scanty, but the activity attributed to them is an important witness to the degree to which they participated freely in society.

The first passage is one which reports that the doorkeeper of the "palace" of Ishbosheth, Saul's son and successor on the throne of the northern tribes, was a woman. The notation is one of the details included in the description of the assassination of Ishbosheth:

> Now the sons of Rimmon the Beerothite, Rechab and Baanah, set out, and about the heat of the day they came to the house of Ishbosheth, as he was taking his noonday rest. And behold, the doorkeeper of the house had been cleaning wheat, but she grew drowsy and slept; so Rechab and Baanah his brother slipped in. (II Sam. 4:5f.)

And beheaded the king.

It is a bucolic scene. The royal palace was simply a house. There was a concièrge at the door who also had domestic duties. The pressure of affairs of state was so great that the king met them prone. When the guardian of the doorway followed her master's example, the regicides slipped in. One of the pleasures of a vivid imagination is pondering what would have happened had she remained awake. A battle royal?

Four narratives describe women appealing directly to the king, either for help or for justice. One of them, which has been discussed in another connection here, reports the use of a wise woman from Tekoa to persuade David to clarify the status of Absalom by presenting David with a fictitious appeal for justice (II Sam. 14:1–24). A second is the famous report of the prostitute appealing to Solomon when her roommate had stolen her infant and had left her own dead child in its place (I Kings 3:16–28). A third is a grim narrative mentioned earlier in the discussion of the love of Israelite mothers for their children. During a siege of Samaria, famine became so severe that two mothers agreed to eat their children. After the first child had been killed, cooked, and eaten, the mother of the second child concealed her son. The woman whose son had been eaten then appealed to the king for justice (II Kings 6:24–31).

Still another description of a woman appealing to the king for help has been preserved in the Elisha stories. A widow whose son the prophet had revived had moved to Philistia during a famine in Israel at the suggestion of Elisha. Seven years later, when the famine had left Israel, she returned:

> And at the end of the seven years, when the woman returned from the land of the Philistines, she went forth to appeal to the king for her house and her land. Now the king was talking with Gehazi the servant of the man of God saying, "Tell me all the great things that Elisha has done." And while he was telling the king how Elisha had restored the dead to life, behold, the woman whose son he had restored

to life appealed to the king for her house and her land. And Gehazi said, "My lord, O king, here is the woman, and here is her son whom Elisha restored to life." And when the king asked the woman, she told him. So the king appointed an official for her, saying, "Restore all that was hers, together with all the produce of the fields from the day that she left the land until now." (II Kings 8:3–6)

We cannot be certain how reliable the picture of the legal rights of the woman reported here is because the power of Elisha seems to be the primary interest of the narrator. But if we take the story as told to represent the legal realities, we have further confirmation that a woman could own land, a house, and the yield of the land. We also again have reported for us an instance of a woman exercising the right to appeal to the king for justice or help.

VI

The evidence surveyed in this chapter is slight in comparison with that available for a reconstruction of the status of the ancient Israelite woman in the home. Nonetheless, we have seen that there are passages which do describe women acting in society outside the home. The relative proportion of the two categories of data indicates that the family was the primary frame of reference for the woman, as it was also for the man. Outside the family, however, we found women being described as moving about freely, as exercising a role of leadership in the village and in the court, as holding personal property, as representing the family in its claim to the title to land, as engaging in economic activities, and as appealing to the king for justice.

At no point in the Old Testament are we given explicit answers to our questions about the role and status of woman. We have to deduce this from the evidence preserved for us for reasons having nothing to do with our questions. From that evidence, however, it now seems proper to conclude that the assessment proposed earlier here continues to stand. Women had a primary role in ancient Israelite society of the utmost importance. This role was the bearing and raising of children. It was a role essential for the survival of the people. By its nature, it was carried on within the family. There, the husband and wife were differentiated biologically but appear to have been granted equality within the differentiation.

Outside the home, women seem to have had access to nearly every activity we normally associate with men. We will find the single exception to this in the next chapter. The fact that fewer women than men ruled is most easily explained by the more dangerous and demanding role of woman within the family than by any hypothesis of the repression of woman in ancient Israel. Such a hypothesis makes the evidence of their participation in government and in the economy virtually inexplicable.

CHAPTER 9

Women in the Cult

I

A segment of the scholarly community has long held that women were virtually excluded from the worship of the God of Israel. It is alleged that their deities were the gods and goddesses of fertility. Georg Beer wrote:

> Only a few religious leaders appear among the names of women in the Old Testament. This is due to the deliberate exclusion of women from the public cult. The religion of Israel, and also of Judaism, was in general a man's religion. For this reason, the oldest laws of worship (Ex. 23:17; 34:23; Deut. 16:16) explicitly address themselves only to the men and demand of them at least three appearances at the shrine yearly at festivals corresponding to our three major festivals, Easter, Pentecost, and Harvest Festival.[63]

Since ancient Israel had a theocentric culture, participation in the public cult is a crucial index of status. The Old Testament reports the official cult as the veneration of the Lord and describes the worship of all other gods as apostasy. The status of woman in the Old Testament will be heavily dependent on her participation in the worship of the Lord. If Beer's statement be correct, the provisional conclusions defended thus far will have to be altered significantly.

The importance of the issue of women's participation in worship has long been recognized, and it has been reviewed carefully in Ismar J. Peritz' "Women in the Ancient Hebrew Cult," and in Clarence J. Vos's *Woman in Old Testament Worship*. This presentation will examine the evidence under four major categories: women as members of the sacred congregation, women as officials in the cult, the participation of women in cultic events, and the standing of women before the Lord.

II

The presence of women when "the people of the LORD" appeared in God's presence is basic to the standing of women in the cult. If they were excluded, it is difficult to see how they could have had anything but second-class standing. If they were present, then the possibility exists that they may have participated in other ways.

As Beer pointed out, Ex. 23:17; 34:23; and Deut. 16:16 stipulate that all males must appear before the Lord three times each year: "Three times in the year shall all your males appear before the LORD God, the God of Israel" (Ex. 34:23; see also ch. 23:17). Deuteronomy 16:16 adds the names of the festivals: "at the feast of unleavened bread, at the feast of weeks, and at the feast of booths." If these passages alone be considered, we would have reason to believe that women had no place in the sacred congregation.

Other passages, however, attest to the presence of women. Deuteronomy 29:10–13 describes a solemn convocation of all the people of God gathered to make (or to renew) its covenant with the Lord. Wives are explicitly mentioned as being present (v. 11). Deuteronomy 31:12 stipulates that wives are to participate in the Festival of Booths (see vs. 10f.), even though they were not mentioned in Deut. 16:16 (cited earlier here): "Assemble the people, men, women, and little ones, and the sojourner within your towns, that they may hear and learn to fear the LORD your God, and be careful to do all the words of this law."

After the Babylonian exile, a solemn convocation of all the people was held in Jerusalem. "And Ezra the priest brought the law before the assembly, both men and women and all who could hear with understanding, on the first day of the seventh month" (Neh. 8:2). It then was read. Presumably, "all who could hear with understanding" meant children old enough to comprehend, although it might refer to those who knew enough Hebrew to understand. The solemnity of the occasion is clear. This is the sacred congregation, the whole of the people of God. It also is clear that women were included.

Two other post-exilic passages also state that women were members of the holy convocation. One passage is an oracle proclaimed by Joel in which the people are summoned into God's presence during a plague of locusts (Joel 2:16). Not only were brides summoned, but also nursing infants. Their presence would have made for an unruly congregation unless their nurses were there also! Finally, a late commentary on the Deuteronomic history (Judges, Samuel, Kings) reports that Jehoshaphat and "all the men of Judah" appeared in the temple to appeal for divine help during an attack by Moabites and Ammonites. They were joined by "their little ones, their wives, and their children" (II Chron. 20:13).

The dates of these passages vary. The three laws that mention men only are very old. Exodus 23:17 is from the Covenant Code, the oldest of the law codes. Exodus

34:23 is from the ritual decalogue which now is part of
the Yahwist source, the oldest narrative strand in the
Pentateuch. Deuteronomy 16:16 belongs to the original
Deuteronomic law code. However, vs. 10f. of ch. 16,
which includes women among the participants in the
Feast of Weeks, is of the same date as Deut. 16:16. The
other passages cited are from after 586 B.C.

III

There were no priestesses in ancient Israel. The feminine form of the word for priest does not appear in the
Hebrew Old Testament. This, however, is the only cultic
office reserved to the male. Since other peoples in the
ancient Near East worshiped in cults which used priestesses, their absence in the Yahwism of ancient Israel
must have been deliberate. Explanations have been offered for this,[64] but all are conjectural.

Several cultic offices were held by women. One of
them, servitor at the door of the Tent of Meeting, is
mentioned twice. In the older reference, women servi-
tors were involved in a scandal: "Now Eli was very old,
and he heard all that his sons were doing to all Israel, and
how they lay with the women who served at the entrance
to the tent of meeting" (I Sam. 2:22). The later reference
to this group appears in the P stratum in the Pentateuch
in the midst of the description of the manufacturing of
the implements for the tabernacle (Ex. 38:8). Neither
passage tells us what this group normally did, and once
again scholarly conjecture has ranged over a wide spec-
trum of possibilities. All are conjectures.

The feminine form of the Hebrew word for prophet
($n^e bi'ah$) is applied to five individuals in the Old Testament. One of them is the wife of the prophet Isaiah (Isa.

8:3). The other prophetesses are Miriam, Deborah, Huldah, and Noadiah.

Miriam, the sister of Moses and Aaron, is called a prophetess in a very old passage in which she is described as leading a victory song (Ex. 15:20f.). She is mentioned along with her brothers in Micah 6:3f., a late passage. The longest reference to her as a prophetess reports a family squabble in which she and Aaron base their protest to Moses' Cushite wife on their prophetic authority (Num. 12:1–8). This evoked a divine response which subordinated them to Moses without denying their prophetic standing:

> Hear my words: If there is a prophet among you, I the LORD make myself known to him in a vision, I speak with him in a dream. Not so with my servant Moses; he is entrusted with all my house. With him I speak mouth to mouth, clearly, and not in dark speech; and he beholds the form of the LORD. Why then were you not afraid to speak against my servant Moses? (Vs. 6–8)

The activity of Deborah is reported both in an ancient victory song (Judg., ch.5) and in a later prose version (ch. 4). She is called a prophetess in the prose version (ch. 4:4). It continues:

> She sent and summoned Barak the son of Abinoam from Kedesh in Naphtali, and said to him, "The LORD, the God of Israel, commands you, 'Go, gather your men at Mount Tabor, taking ten thousand from the tribe of Naphtali and the tribe of Zebulun. And I will draw out Sisera, the general of Jabin's army, to meet you by the river Kishon with his chariots and his troops; and I will give him into your hand.' "
> (Judg. 4:6f.)

When the Israelites had mustered out, "Deborah said to Barak, 'Up! For this is the day in which the LORD has given Sisera into your hand. Does not the LORD go out before you?' " (v. 14). In both oracles, Deborah is reported as speaking and acting as the Deuteronomic historians elsewhere picture male prophets as speaking and acting (see I Sam. 15:2f.; I Kings 12:22–24; 22:6, 15–17; II Kings 3:16–20; 13:14–19; 20:13f.). We cannot here enter the discussion of the differences, if there were any, between these prophets and such figures as Amos, Hosea, Isaiah, and Jeremiah. It will have to suffice to say that the Deuteronomic historians felt it proper to identify Deborah as a prophetess, and to describe her as acting in precisely the same way as six male prophets are reported to have functioned.

Huldah is the major prophetess. A law code which contained ominous threats had been found during the remodeling of the Temple. King Josiah ordered its finders to consult a prophet about it:

> So Hilkiah the priest, and Ahikam, and Achbor, and Shaphan, and Asaiah went to Huldah the prophetess, the wife of Shallum the son of Tikvah, son of Harhas, keeper of the wardrobe (now she dwelt in Jerusalem in the Second Quarter); and they talked with her. And she said to them, "Thus says the LORD, the God of Israel, 'Tell the man who sent you to me, Thus says the LORD, Behold, I will bring evil upon this place and upon its inhabitants, all the words of the book which the king of Judah has read. . . . But as to the king of Judah, who sent you to inquire of the LORD, thus shall you say to him, Thus says the LORD, the God of Israel. . . . Therefore, behold, I will gather you to your fathers, and you shall be gathered to your grave in peace, and your eyes shall not see all the evil which I will bring upon this place.' " (II Kings 22:14–26)

Huldah was married, yet she was known in her own right as the most reliable prophetic figure in Jerusalem, even though Jeremiah had begun to prophesy in 626, five years before this consultation. Her words were preserved, even though her prediction about the way Josiah would die proved to be wrong, and she used the same words to introduce her oracles as did Jeremiah (compare II Kings 22:15f. with Jer. 2:2, 5; 4:3; 6:9; etc.). It is clear that Huldah was a major cult official, and her reputation in her own time probably was greater than Jeremiah's.[65]

The prophetess Noadiah is mentioned as one of those who opposed Nehemiah's rebuilding Jerusalem after the exile (Neh. 6:14), and an oracle by a post-exilic prophet simply assumes the presence of both female and male prophets:

> And it shall come to pass afterward,
> that I will pour out my spirit on all flesh;
> your sons and your daughters shall prophesy,
> your old men shall dream dreams,
> and your young men shall see visions.
>
> (Joel 2:28)

Miriam and Deborah are also described as cult singers (Ex. 15:20f.; Judg. 5:12). Other examples of this role will be reported later here in another context.

The data mentioning Israelite women as personnel in non-Yahwist cults falls primarily into three categories: cult prostitutes, witches (or necromancers), and mourners for alien gods. The first of these seems to be a part of the basis for the claim that "pure Yahwism" was primarily a man's religion, since cult prostitutes served either in Baalism or in a debased Yahwism.

There are two terms in Biblical Hebrew for prostitute. *Zonah,* a feminine participle from the verb meaning "to fornicate," appears twenty-six times in the Old Testament. A *zonah* could be what we today would call a prostitute, or she could be a participant in ritual promiscuity (as, apparently, in Hos. 4:13f., to be quoted below). *Qᵉdeshah* is the feminine form of a noun designating a cult prostitute. It is formed from the same root from which the Hebrew term "holy" *(qadosh)* comes. The feminine form of the term for cult prostitute appears five

times in the Old Testament (Gen. 38:21 [twice], 22;
Deut. 23:17; Hos. 4:14). The masculine form appears six
times (Deut. 23:17; I Kings 14:24; 15:12; 22:46; II Kings
23:7; Job 36:14): The book of The Proverbs uses the
phrase "foreign woman" to refer to a promiscuous
woman who might also be a prostitute.

The frequency with which the technical term for cult
prostitute appears in the Old Testament is almost
equally divided between male and female functionaries.
Deuteronomy 23:17 indicates the evenhandedness of the
condemnation of the office: "There shall be no cult prostitute of the daughters of Israel, neither shall there be a
cult prostitute of the sons of Israel." Hosea 4:14, which
is earlier than the Deuteronomic legislation just quoted,
uses both *zonah* and *q^edeshah:*

I will not punish your daughters when they play the harlot
     [*zonah*],
     nor your brides when they commit adultery;
for the men themselves go aside with harlots [*zonah*],
     and sacrifice with cult prostitutes [*q^edeshah*],
and a people without understanding shall come to ruin.

Genesis 38:15–22, part of the story of the patriarch Judah
and his daughter-in-law Tamar, also uses *zonah* and
q^edeshah interchangeably. Judah is said to have thought
Tamar to be a *zonah* in v. 15, but he and his men refer
to her as a *q^edeshah* three times in vs. 21f. This narrative,
incidentally, is the oldest of the passages being reported
here.

The evidence available suggests that there were both
female and male cult prostitutes attached to shrines in
Palestine in Old Testament times. Both men and women
participated in a cult in which sexual intercourse was a
part. Such ritual promiscuity and the cult personnel used
in it were condemned by spokesmen for strict Yahwism
at least from the time of Hosea onward. An estimate of

the prevalence of the cult based upon the frequency of the appearance of the terms for cult prostitutes alone would be wrong. Allusions to it using other than the technical vocabulary cited here (such as Jer. 3:2f. where *zonah* is used), and the prevalence of figurines of the mother goddess in excavations of Israelite cities, indicate that the cult was widespread. The evidence of the appearance of the term for cult prostitute (both female and male) makes it clear that both men and women participated in cultic promiscuity. Therefore an inference sometimes drawn from the presence of fertility worship, that it was primarily a cult for women, must be rejected.

A second kind of non-Yahwist cult leadership in which women participated is reported to us in Lev. 20:27: "A man or a woman who is a medium or a wizard shall be put to death; they shall be stoned with stones, their blood shall be upon them." This is one of several references to the worship of ancestors in the Old Testament. The calling up of the dead was done to gain knowledge of the future. If the spirits of the dead had accurate knowledge of the future, it was because they controlled it. Such authority over the course of future events conflicted with the belief that the Lord ruled the people's history. Thus the worship of ancestors, or necromancy, was another cult competing with Yahwism in ancient Israel.

I Samuel 28:3–25 reports how the cult operated and confirms the role of women in it. As the story opens, Saul is facing a major battle with the Philistines. Saul's strict Yahwism is reported to us in the comment that he had expelled the mediums and wizards, the personnel of the cult of the dead, from the land (v. 3). Samuel, who had earlier mediated to Saul the word of the Lord about the future, had died. The inference is that Saul had no guidance about the outcome of the impending battle. In his urgency, Saul turned to a necromancer to bring back the dead Samuel, hoping to get from him information about the Lord's plan for the battle. This, by the way, may be an accurate report of the way in which the essentially competing religions in the land constantly fused into unstable union.

The story is eerie. Our concern, however, is not with the degree to which it reflects religious practices in early Israelite history. We are concerned solely with the fact that the cult official was a woman, the well-known Witch of Endor. In an hour of national crisis, the king turned for help to a female cult official, just as Josiah and his court turned to the prophetess Huldah during a later and different crisis.

Other bits and pieces of information about the role of women in non-Yahwist cults have survived in the Old Testament, but they are too fragmentary to be very clear. The strangest is Ezek. 13:18f.:

> Thus says the Lord GOD: Woe to the women who sew magic bands upon all wrists, and make veils for the heads of persons of every stature, in the hunt for souls! Will you hunt down souls belonging to my people, and keep other souls alive for your own profit? You have profaned me among my people for handfuls of barley and for pieces of bread, putting to death persons who should not die and keeping alive persons who should not live, by your lies to my people, who listen to lies.

Walther Eichrodt probably is correct in seeing here Israelite equivalents to magical practices described in more detail in Babylonian sources.[66]

Ezekiel also described women sitting beside the north entrance to the Temple "weeping for Tammuz" (Ezek. 8:14). This was probably ritual lamentation in the cult of a dying-rising god of fertility. Jeremiah 44:15–19 reports that Israelite women burned incense to "the Queen of Heaven" (the Canaanite Astarte), poured out libations to her, and made cakes displaying her likeness. II Kings

23:7 reports that women "wove hangings for the Asherah" which were put in the quarters of male cult prostitutes.

The passages we have just reviewed demonstrate that Israelite women served as personnel in the worship of the Lord and in other cults. Women are also reported as participating in the rites of the cult even when they are not described as cult personnel. In reviewing this evidence, note that none of these acts of worship is reported to have been restricted to females only. We are again dealing with passages in which men and women are described as engaging in the same actions.

It seems reasonable to believe that a theophany, a divine visitation, was a very important cult event. Such visitations are reported at important points in the Old Testament, such as just before the giving of the law at Sinai (Ex., ch. 19) or at the time a person became a prophet (Isa., ch. 6). In my opinion, it would be difficult to maintain that women shared fully in the worship of the Lord if they were excluded from this primary cultic event.

There are three reports of women receiving theophanies.[67] Hagar is the recipient of two of them. After she had fled into the desert to get away from Sarah's anger,

> the angel of the LORD found her by a spring of water in the wilderness, the spring on the way to Shur. And he said, "Hagar, maid of Sarai, where have you come from and where are you going?" She said, "I am fleeing from my mistress Sarai." The angel of the LORD said to her, "Return to your mistress, and submit to her." The angel of the LORD also said to her, "I will so greatly multiply your descendants that they cannot be numbered for multitude." And the angel of the LORD said to her, "Behold, you are with child, and shall bear a son; you shall call his name Ishmael, because the LORD has given heed to your affliction. He shall be a wild ass of a man, his hand against every man and every man's hand against him; and he shall dwell over against all his kinsmen."

> So she called the name of the LORD who spoke to her, "Thou art a God of seeing"; for she said, "Have I really seen God and remain alive after seeing him?" (Gen. 16:7–13)

This is the earliest of the narrative strands of the Pentateuch. The second oldest strand also reports a theophany to Hagar after Sarah had her driven out (Gen. 21:17f.). Both of these passages reveal that the two narrators and their auditors took it for granted that a woman could receive a theophany. Only the use of the messenger (the angel) sets the structure of these incidents apart from similar theophanies to Abraham (see Gen. 12:1–3; 15:1–5).

We find a third account of a theophany to a woman in Judg. 13:2–25. Here again, the divine visitation is mediated through an angel. The story opens:

> And there was a certain man of Zorah, of the tribe of the Danites, whose name was Manoah; and his wife was barren and had no children. And the angel of the LORD appeared to the woman and said to her, "Behold, you are barren and have no children; but you shall conceive and bear a son."

When her husband asked God in prayer for a repetition of the visit, the angel was sent a second time, again to the woman (vs. 8f.). Only when she summoned her husband did he participate for the first time in the theophany. The husband's words after the angel had left recall the response of Hagar in Gen. 16:13: "And Manoah said to his wife, 'We shall surely die, for we have seen God!' " (v. 22).

God visited a woman by means of an angelic intermediary in all three accounts. In two of the three (Gen. 16:13 and Judg. 12:22), the visitation is described as a theophany. The third of the stories differs from the first two only in recounting one visitation to the wife alone, followed by a second to both wife and husband. The fundamental significance of these stories is that they

make it clear that the ancient Israelites felt it as appropriate for a woman as for a man to participate in a theophany, the most important of all cultic events.

The experiences of the prophets which started their
careers (such as those reported in Isa. 6:1–8; Jer. 1:4–10;
Ezek., chs. 1 to 3; and Amos 3:8) also were theophanies.
They seem to be the basis of the prophet's right to say,
"Thus says the LORD." If this be valid, we also can infer
that the statement by Huldah, "Thus says the LORD, the
God of Israel: 'Tell the man who sent you to me, Thus
says the LORD . . .' " (II Kings 22:15), implies that she also
had been granted a theophany.

The cult provided various methods for consulting the
Lord. The priest's oracle seems often to have been given
by means of the casting of the sacred lots, the urim and
thummim. The interpretation of dreams and consulting
a prophet also were used. Women as well as men were
free to consult prophets. In the story of Rebekah, we are
told simply that she "went to inquire of the LORD," and
the means used are not given (Gen. 25:22f.). The wife of
Jeroboam I, at his urging, went to consult with a prophet
when her son became ill (I Kings 14:1–18), and the
wealthy Shunammite who had befriended Elisha brought
her dead child to him (II Kings 4:18–37). In all three of
these instances, women inquired of the Lord on behalf of
children, born or unborn. This is further confirmation of
the relationship believed to exist between the role of the
woman as childbearer and the activity of God among the
people of God.

We have already determined that women were included in the sacred congregation that gathered to celebrate the great festivals (see, e.g., Deut. 5:14; 16:10f.).
The passages upon which this conclusion is based, however, do not stipulate the presence of wives and mothers.
This calls for explanation. Three possibilities come to
mind: that the mother was excluded from sacrificial rites

for reasons now lost, that the wife is included in the commandments as a daughter in the extended family in which she could be identified as either daughter or wife, or that the wife was free to attend or to absent herself because of the demands made upon her by child care. The first of these possibilities cannot be discussed since there is no evidence available. The second seems unlikely because of the importance of the wife and mother throughout the Old Testament. There is one important narrative which supports the third possibility.

The story of the birth of Samuel is an early witness to the place of women in strict Yahwist circles. Samuel is the prophet active at the time of the emergence of the monarchy. He became, for later generations struggling against royal tyranny, the epitome of opposition to Canaanite monarchical tendencies. The birth legend has been preserved for us by Deuteronomic historians, a later but strict Yahwist circle. Thus the birth narrative may report not only early Yahwist attitudes but also the views of Yahwism in the sixth and fifth centuries B.C.

Hannah, the barren wife, prays urgently for a son, promising to dedicate him to the Lord if her prayer is heard. She is heard and bears a son whom she names Samuel:

> And the man Elkanah and all his house went up to offer to the Lord the yearly sacrifice, and to pay his vow. But Hannah did not go up, for she said to her husband, "As soon as the child is weaned, I will bring him, that he may appear in the presence of the Lord, and abide there for ever." And Elkanah her husband said to her, "Do what seems best to you, wait until you have weaned him; only, may the Lord establish his word." (I Sam. 1:21–23)

When Samuel had been weaned and presented to Eli to serve the Lord under him at Shiloh, Hannah resumed going to the shrine with the rest of the family (I Sam. 2:19).

The narrative tends to confirm the conjecture that the absence of the wife and mother from the list of those expected to be present at the great feasts may have been due to the demands of childbearing. If this single example can be taken to reflect custom, the wife was allowed to remain home at her own discretion until the child had been weaned. This receives further support from the summons of "even nursing infants" in Joel 2:15f. to an extraordinary convocation before the Lord.

We have explicit evidence that daughters, maidservants, and widows were included in the celebration of the Sabbath, the Festival of Weeks, and the Festival of Booths. Thus woman as such was not excluded. The legend of Samuel's birth (and Joel 2:15f.) suggests further that mothers were excused from participation because of the demands of childbearing. Obviously, therefore, the great festivals were not cult events for men only.[68]

Women are portrayed twice in the Old Testament as initiating a cultic occasion. The first is reported as part of Jezebel's plot to kill Naboth and take his family's inheritance. Her instructions for the trumped-up trial were: "Proclaim a fast, and set Naboth on high among the people; and set two base fellows opposite him, and let them bring a charge against him, saying, 'You have cursed God and the king.' Then take him out, and stone him to death" (I Kings 21:9f.). This, of course, was a special event. The Book of Esther, however, reports that Esther and Mordecai instituted the Feast of Purim:

> Then Queen Esther, the daughter of Abihail, and Mordecai the Jew gave full written authority, confirming this second letter about Purim. Letters were sent to all the Jews, to the hundred and twenty-seven provinces of the kingdom of

Ahasuerus, in words of peace and truth, that these days of Purim should be observed at their appointed seasons, as Mordecai the Jew and Queen Esther enjoined upon the Jews, and as they had laid down for themselves and for their descendants, with regard to their fasts and their lamenting. The command of Queen Esther fixed these practices of Purim, and it was recorded in writing. (Esth. 9:29–32)

Sacrifice was an important part of the cult in ancient Israel. A priest normally officiated, and the Priestly Code of the Pentateuch elaborates his role in great detail. All Yahwist priests were male. To the degree, therefore, that we discuss officiating at a sacrifice, we describe an exclusively male cult act. This also, however, is a cultic act from which the majority of men were excluded. Their part in the sacrifice was the right to bring offerings and to receive the appropriate benefits. When we discuss sacrifice as a rite in which a worshiper made use of a priest, we find that women could sacrifice as well as could men.

Several different steps were involved in sacrifice. At least three can be distinguished today: the presentation of the offering to the priest, the preparation and offering up of the sacrifice by the priest on behalf of the worshiper, and the sacred meal in which the worshiper ate designated parts of certain sacrifices at the shrine. When we ask about the participation of women (and of the average male Israelite), we are asking whether or not women could present sacrifices and whether or not they could eat the appropriate parts of certain sacrifices after they had been offered up by a priest.

The story of the birth of Samuel just cited provides a report of a woman bringing a sacrifice:

And when she [Hannah] had weaned him, she took him up with her, along with a three-year-old bull, an ephah of flour, and a skin of wine; and she brought him to the house of the

LORD at Shiloh; and the child was young. Then they slew the bull, and they brought the child to Eli. (I Sam. 1:24f.)

Presumably, the personnel of the shrine killed the bull. The legend of the birth of Samson, cited earlier here as an instance of a theophany to a woman, reports that husband and wife together offered the sacrifice at the conclusion of the theophany (Judg. 13:15–20). No priest is reported as being present.

The narrative of Hannah offering a sacrifice is confirmed by legislation which specifies the obligation of a woman to bring a sacrifice under certain circumstances. The best-known of these laws are those which end her "uncleanness" following childbirth:

> And when the days of her purifying are completed, whether for a son or for a daughter, she shall bring to the priest at the door of the tent of meeting a lamb a year old for a burnt offering, and a young pigeon or a turtledove for a sin offering, and he shall offer it before the LORD, and make atonement for her; then she shall be clean from the flow of her blood. This is the law for her who bears a child, either male or female. (Lev. 12:6f.)

Should she be unable to afford a lamb, two pigeons or two turtledoves can be substituted (v. 8). One writer has observed that the *'adam* and *nephesh* used in Leviticus prior to ch. 12 (where sacrifices appropriate to a woman are described) to refer to the persons bringing sacrifices have a generic force and mean mankind.[69] Even without accepting this, we have ample evidence that women regularly brought sacrifices.

It also is clear that they ate the part of the sacrifice returned to the person bringing it. When the childless Hannah wept during the sacrifice at Shiloh, "Elkanah, her husband, said to her, 'Hannah, why do you weep? And why do you not eat? And why is your heart sad? Am I not more to you than ten sons?' " (I Sam. 1:8). Certain parts of some sacrifices were reserved for the priest. Numbers 18:19 specifies that the priest's daughters could share such food: "All the holy offerings which the people of Israel present to the Lord I give to you, and to your sons and daughters with you, as a perpetual due; it is a covenant of salt for ever before the Lord for you and for your offspring with you." (See also Lev. 10:14f.; 22:12f. Lev. 7:31–35 seems to restrict access to the holy food to the priest and his sons only.)

A vow is a binding promise made to God. The ability to make a vow is a convenient index of the individual's status in the cult. Only those accorded standing before God could make a vow either to God or in the Lord's presence, and only those who had some autonomy could make a vow with a measure of assurance that they would be able to fulfill it.

At least three passages in the Old Testament bear on the ability of a woman to make a vow. One of them is restrictive:

> When a man vows a vow to the Lord, or swears an oath to bind himself by a pledge, he shall not break his word; he shall do according to all that proceeds out of his mouth. Or when a woman vows a vow to the Lord, and binds herself with a pledge, while within her father's house, in her youth, and her father hears of her vow and of her pledge by which she has bound herself, and says nothing to her; then all her vows shall stand, and every pledge by which she has bound herself shall stand. But if her father expresses disapproval to her on the day that he hears of it, no vow of hers, no pledge by which she has bound herself, shall stand; and the Lord will forgive her, because her father opposed her. (Num. 30:2–5)

Verses 6 to 8 assign the father's role to the husband of a married woman, but v. 9 asserts that "any vow of a widow or of a divorced woman, anything by which she has bound herself, shall stand against her." Thus all

women could make vows. Vows made by a woman living
in a family with a male head could be voided by that male
if he acted on the same day on which he learned of the
vow. Women were held accountable for all vows not so
voided.

This law can be given various interpretations. It could
be alleged to reflect the belief that women are capable of
thoughtless decisions, or that a woman had the right to
make any vow she wished (even if she did not always have
the right to keep it!). The vow of Hannah, reported as
having been made without the knowledge or consent of
Elkanah (I Sam. 1:11), has been cited as evidence that
Num. 30:2–15 is a late law representing a restriction of
the greater autonomy once given women.[70]

It might be well to remember the magnitude of the
vows that were possible. Numbers 6:1–6 specifies that
both men and women could take the vow to become a
Nazirite and thus to espouse an ascetic life, and Judg.
11:30 reports Jephthah's vow to sacrifice the first living
being he met upon returning home after a battle. A wife's
vow of chastity could prevent "building up the family's
name" unless her husband took a second wife. No such
consequences for a family would follow upon a vow made
by either a widow or a divorcée.

We probably are not far from the truth, therefore, in
concluding that the partial power of father or husband to
void a woman's vow reflects more the primacy of the
family in ancient Israel than an inferior status of woman
before the Lord. The absence of a law protecting the
right of a wife to void a husband's vow suggests an ine-
quality within the family, as does the husband's right to
void a wife's vow. But the woman's capacity to make
vows, and her ability to keep vows once made and not
voided, indicate that she had standing in the cult.

Prayer is mentioned fairly often in the Old Testament,
although the liturgical laws neither describe it nor pre-

scribe for it. Solomon is pictured as praying on behalf of the nation at the time of the dedication of the royal chapel in Jerusalem (I Kings 8:22–54 = II Chron. 6: 12 to 7:1), and Jeremiah prayed for the people (Jer. 7:16; 11:14; 14:11; 37:3).

One of the few instances of private prayer is in the story of the birth of Samuel. After the annual family sacrifice had been offered up and eaten,

> she [Hannah] was deeply distressed and prayed to the LORD, and wept bitterly. . . . As she continued praying before the LORD, Eli observed her mouth. Hannah was speaking in her heart; only her lips moved, and her voice was not heard; therefore Eli took her to be a drunken woman. And Eli said to her, "How long will you be drunken? Put away your wine from you." But Hannah answered, "No, my lord, I am a woman sorely troubled; I have drunk neither wine nor strong drink, but I have been pouring out my soul before the LORD." (I Sam. 1:10, 12–15)

Eli thought Hannah to be drunken, a detail in the story probably intended to underscore the intensity of her praying. The tale of the contest in fertility between Leah and Rachel contains hints that women may often have prayed intensely for children (Gen. 29:33; 30:17). It seems likely also that some form of prayer accompanied sacrifice, and thus we perhaps should picture women offering up prayers each time they have an offering to present.

Since circumcision was performed only on males in ancient Israel, we would expect that it would have been the exclusive domain of men; yet one of the two narratives describing it reports a woman officiating:

> At a lodging place on the way the LORD met him [Moses] and sought to kill him. Then Zipporah took a flint and cut off her son's foreskin, and touched Moses' feet with it, and said, "Surely you are a bridegroom of blood to me!" So he let him

alone. Then it was that she said, "You are a bridegroom of blood" because of the circumcision. (Ex. 4:24–26)

The passage is murky. The Revised Standard Version inserts Moses' name into the phrase "touched Moses' feet with it," and this adds clarity. Our interest in the verses is confined here to the fact that a woman performed the rite. No explanation of her doing it is given, and we are not told why she had the right to do it. Zipporah was the daughter of the priest of Midian. It might be argued that Moses' intimacy with her violated some sanctity attached to her person which could be removed only by the rite. But this is only conjecture. The other story in which circumcision plays an important part is the report of the rape of Dinah (Gen. ch. 34). Nothing is said there about women participating in the rite.

Women are reported as mourning for the dead several times. David handed over the male descendants of Saul to the Gibeonites. They then executed them to avenge Saul's attack earlier in Gibeon. Thereupon Rizpah, the mother of two of the men, "took sackcloth, and spread it for herself on the rock, from the beginning of harvest until rain fell upon them from the heavens; and she did not allow the birds of the air to come upon them by day, or the beasts of the field by night" (II Sam. 21:10f.). Rizpah's mourning attests to the enormity of David's offense against the family of Saul. Shamed by it, David made what amends he could. He gathered the bones of Saul and Jonathan, and the bones of the other sons of Saul, and gave them a proper burial (vs. 11–14).

Other forms of mourning for the dead (excluding songs of lamentation which will be reported separately) included cutting off the hair (Isa. 3:24; Amos 8:10) and beating the breast (Nahum 2:7). If we include women in legislation addressed to "the sons of the LORD your God," as we have found reason to do several times in this study, we might add laceration (Deut. 14:1), although all other references to this in the Old Testament seem to be confined to men only (e.g., I Kings 18:28; Jer. 16:6; 41:5; 47:5; etc.). We would expect to find most of the rites of mourning shared by both men and women. Presumably the mourners were the survivors, rather than men or women only.

We have already had references describing Miriam and Deborah as singers (Ex. 15:20f.; Judg. 5:12). This role continues throughout the Old Testament. One of the pro-David incidents inserted into the report of the reign of Saul pictures women as chanting,

> Saul has slain his thousands,
> and David his ten thousands.
> (I Sam. 18:7)

In the late post-exilic period, the Chronicler reported that both the sons and daughters of Heman were temple musicians (I Chron. 25:5f.). Elsewhere the Chronicler speaks of singing men and women (II Chron. 35:25). At this late date, any attempt to assign a specific musical function to one sex or the other is impossible.

Singing songs of lamentation, however, seems to have been primarily the domain of women. The lament over the death of Saul is attributed to David, but the act of lamentation reported in it is assigned to women:

> Ye daughters of Israel, weep over Saul,
>   who clothed you daintily in scarlet,
>   who put ornaments of gold upon your apparel.
> (II Sam. 1:24)

Several centuries later, Jeremiah mentioned women who were especially skilled in lamentation (Jer. 9:17–21), and Ezekiel repeated the picture of women singing laments a few years later (Ezek. 32:16). Since the Lord was believed to be acting in a woman's womb to bring new life to the people of God, it was appropriate that those same women should be the ones who mourned before the Lord on behalf of the people at a time of death.

Thus, far from finding women to have been excluded from the worship of Yahweh, we have seen evidence that they participated in many different roles and in many cult acts. They are never described as having served as priests. All other offices in the cult, and all cult acts other than the technical acts involved in offering up the sacrifice, are attributed in the Old Testament both to men and to women. We can only conclude, therefore, that women were full participants in the worship of the Lord.

IV

Because women participated fully in the veneration of God, we may conclude that they, like men, had standing in God's sight. Thus they could be judged righteous or sinful. In strictures against apostasy, men and women are treated alike:

> If your brother, the son of your mother, or your son, or your daughter, or the wife of your bosom, or your friend who is as your own soul, entices you secretly, saying, "Let us go and serve other gods," which neither you nor your fathers have known, some of the gods of the peoples that are round about you, whether near you or far off from you, from the one end of the earth to the other, you shall not yield to him or listen to him, nor shall your eye pity him, nor shall you spare him, nor shall you conceal him; but you shall kill him; your hand shall be first against him to put him to death, and afterwards the hand of all the people. You shall stone him to death with stones, because he sought to draw you away from the LORD your God, who brought you out of the land of Egypt, out of the house of bondage. (Deut. 13:6–10)

Here again, incidentally, we find the masculine singular pronoun taking both men and women as antecedents.[71]

We do need, however, to give special attention to material which describes women as unclean. Such passages fall into five categories according to the cause: diseases, bodily discharges, childbirth, contact with the dead, and sexual intercourse.

In four of the five categories, men and women are dealt with alike. Laws prescribing the diagnosis of diseases making one unclean and stipulating the rites of purification seem to have applied to men and women without distinction. A regulation from Leviticus is an example of this:

> When a man or woman has a disease on the head or the beard, the priest shall examine the disease; and if it appears deeper than the skin, and the hair in it is yellow and thin, then the priest shall pronounce him unclean; it is an itch, a leprosy of the head or the beard. And if the priest examines the itching disease, and it appears no deeper than the skin and there is no black hair in it, then the priest shall shut up the person with the itching disease for seven days. . . . (Lev. 13:29–31; see also ch. 12:38f.)

Leviticus, ch. 15, describes the ritual condition of those who have had a bodily discharge and prescribes for their cleansing. The discharges of both male and female are described. In both cases, all that the unclean person has touched becomes unclean (vs. 2–12 for the man and vs. 19–27 for the woman). Both are unclean for seven days (vs. 13 and 28), but the man only is required to wash his clothes and bathe. On the eighth day, the man

> shall take two turtledoves or two young pigeons, and come before the LORD to the door of the tent of meeting, and give them to the priest; and the priest shall offer them, one for a sin offering and the other for a burnt offering; and the

priest shall make atonement for him before the LORD for his discharge (vs. 14f.).

With the exception of a change of the pronoun referring to the person bringing the offering, the ritual prescribed for the woman is precisely the same (vs. 29f.):

Uncleanness following childbirth involved only the mother:

> If a woman conceives, and bears a male child, then she shall be unclean seven days; as at the time of her menstruation, she shall be unclean. And on the eighth day the flesh of his foreskin shall be circumcised. Then she shall continue for thirty-three days in the blood of her purifying; she shall not touch any hallowed thing, nor come into the sanctuary, until the days of her purifying are completed. But if she bears a female child, then she shall be unclean two weeks, as in her menstruation; and she shall continue in the blood of her purifying for sixty-six days. (Lev. 12:2–5)

Thus the mother is twice as "unclean" following the birth of a daughter as she is after the birth of a son. However, the same offering is to be made for son or daughter after the period of purification has ended. Martin Noth observed: "The sexual processes, especially birth, were also reckoned 'unclean' far beyond the circle of Israel, because mysterious powers were seen to be at work in them, having little or no connection with the official cults."[72] This is not an entirely satisfactory explanation for a literature which elsewhere views Yahweh, the God of Israel, as intimately active in all stages of birth from conception to delivery. The mother's uncleanness may have been the result of the afterbirth being regarded as a bodily emission, or the woman who had just given birth to an infant may have been "unclean" because she had been too closely involved with the work of deity. She would need a period to be de-energized, so to speak; and that period would need to be twice as long for the birth of a child which might become capable in its turn of bearing children as for a male child. This the law specifies.

Contact with a dead body defiled man and woman alike. The law specifying purification following contact with a dead body seems at first sight to apply only to males (Num. 19:11–22). We have already seen examples in which the masculine singular personal pronoun assumes bisexual antecedents, as well as passages (e.g., Gen. 1:27) in which *'adam* (man) means humanity. Numbers 5:1–4, a law dealing primarily with leprosy, specifies that "every one that is unclean through contact with the dead; you shall put out both male and female, putting them outside the camp, that they may not defile their camp, in the midst of which I dwell" (vs. 2b, 3). Thus we would seem to be justified in concluding that the laws of purification after contact with a dead body in Num., ch. 19, applied to men and women in precisely the same way.

Two narratives imply that uncleanness was associated with sexual intercourse. The people are commanded, "Do not go near a woman," in preparation for the theophany at Mt. Sinai (Ex. 19:15). Many years later, when David requested of a priest food for his band,

> the priest answered David, "I have no common bread at hand, but there is holy bread; if only the young men have kept themselves from women." And David answered the priest, "Of a truth women have been kept from us as always when I go on an expedition; the vessels of the young men are holy, even when it is a common journey; how much more today will their vessels be holy?" (I Sam. 21:4f.)

These two narratives appear to be illustrations of the law found in Lev. 15:18: "If a man lies with a woman and has an emission of semen, both of them shall bathe themselves in water, and be unclean until evening." Thus the impurity present in sexual intercourse was the contact

with a man's bodily emission. It was not the woman who
made the male unclean, but rather the male who made
both himself and the woman unclean.[73]

Thus the uncleanness of woman essentially parallels
that of man. Both were unclean by reason of some kinds
of illness or because of the bodily emissions characteristic of their sex. Both became unclean if they touched a
corpse. Since a male bodily emission occurs during sexual intercourse, and since contact by others with either
a man's or a woman's bodily emission defiled them, sexual intercourse defiled. The one form of uncleanness
restricted to woman was that which followed childbirth.
It was suggested here that this uncleanness may have
been a result of too close a contact with God.

V

Little more needs to be added. Woman in ancient
Israel seems to have participated fully in the worship of
the Lord, to have had standing in God's sight equal to
that given the man, and to have borne no unusual onus
of uncleanness. In other words, the woman's status in the
cult was equal to that of the man. The single exception
to this is the role of the priest. We saw in an earlier
chapter, however, that women had had reserved to them
their own unique and crucial kind of intimacy with God:
the bearing of children. This status seems to reappear
once more in the laws of ritual uncleanness.

CHAPTER 10

Female Personifications

I

Two kinds of data in the Old Testament referring to women will not be discussed: names of women in genealogies and moral standards involving women. Much of the information that would be used for each topic has already appeared in other connections, and a discussion of these themes would be repetitious. For example, one important category of data dealing with women in genealogies is the names of queens and queen mothers. This has already been discussed. Most of the basic ethical standards which involve women as women, that is, sexual ethics and the relationships of husband and wife, parents and children, also have been presented. Some new material, such as the condemnations of bestiality (Lev. 18:23; 20:15f.; Deut. 27:21), homosexuality (Lev. 18:22; 20:13), and transvestism (Deut. 22:5) could be given, but it is so obviously related to themes already discussed here that this information would not greatly advance our knowledge of the status of woman.

Passages in which nations and attributes of deity are personified as women, however, have not been presented. The description of the latter category is also the appropriate place to raise the question of the gender of God.

II

Passages in which peoples and nations are personified as women can be grouped into those in which the nation is called a daughter, or a virgin daughter, those in which the title is shortened simply to "the virgin Israel," and those in which the nation is referred to either by a feminine personal pronoun or by a feminine attribute.

The title "daughter of Zion" is used in several ways. In Isa. 16:1f. the flight of Moabite refugees to Jerusalem is described:

> They have sent lambs
>   to the ruler of the land,
> from Sela, by way of the desert,
>   to the mount of the daughter of Zion.
> Like fluttering birds,
>   like scattered nestlings,
> so are the daughters of Moab
>   at the fords of the Arnon.

Since the titles "the daughter of Zion" and "the daughters of Moab" appear in the same oracle, its author (either Isaiah or one of his disciples) applied the personification to both the political and the religious capital of his own nation (the daughter of Zion) and to another people (the daughters of Moab).

"The daughter of Zion" appears in four oracles of woe. Three of the four seem to refer only to Jerusalem (often called Zion). After the first Assyrian attack on Judah, when the whole land except Jerusalem had been devastated, Isaiah said,

> And the daughter of Zion is left
> 	like a booth in a vineyard,
> 	like a lodge in a cucumber field,
> 	like a besieged city.
> 					(Isa. 1:8)

Slightly less than a century later, Jeremiah referred to Jerusalem as "the daughter of Zion" in predicting an attack against the city (Jer. 6:2–5). A late addition to The Book of Micah, coming from about the same time, employed the term in a warning of the Babylonian exile (Micah 4:9f.). Micah himself, a contemporary of Isaiah, used the title to refer to Jerusalem in an oracle of woe against Lachish (Micah 1:13–16).

Since "daughter of Zion" was used to refer to Jerusalem in oracles of woe, three of which were directed against the city, it is not surprising that it also appears in a lament after its fall:

> Cry aloud to the Lord!
> 	O daughter of Zion!
> Let tears stream down like a torrent
> 	day and night!
> Give yourself no rest,
> 	your eyes no respite!
> 					(Lam. 2:18)

Restoration is promised "the daughter of Zion" in a series of late passages. The tone of these range from militancy to exalted expectation. In Micah 4:13, the hope has martial overtones:

> Arise and thresh,
> 	O daughter of Zion,
> for I will make your horn iron
> 	and your hoofs bronze;
> you shall beat in pieces many peoples,
> 	and shall devote their gain to the LORD,
> 	their wealth to the Lord of the whole earth.

Isaiah 62:11f. is less militant. The simplest statement of hope happens also to be the most inclusive: "Sing and rejoice, O daughter of Zion; for lo, I come and I will dwell in the midst of you, says the LORD" (Zech. 2:10; see also Isa. 4:3f.).

In five oracles, "daughter of Zion" (twice "virgin daughter of Zion") appears in poetic parallelism with "daughters of Jerusalem." Two of the oracles are a taunt song against Assyria attributed to Isaiah (wrongly, in my judgment):

> This is the word that the LORD has spoken concerning him:
>
>> She despises you, she scorns you—
>>> the virgin daughter of Zion;
>> she wags her head behind you—
>>> the daughter of Jerusalem.
>>>> (II Kings 19:21 = Isa. 37:22)

The remaining three passages are oracles of restoration. One seems to have influenced Mark 11:1–10 and its parallels in Matthew and Luke:

> Rejoice greatly, O daughter of Zion!
>> Shout aloud, O daughter of Jerusalem!
> Lo, your king comes to you;
>> triumphant and victorious is he,
> humble and riding on an ass,
>> on a colt the foal of an ass.
>>> (Zech. 9:9)[74]

A series of variations of the title "daughter" appear. These cover much of the same ground that has already been described. The phrase "daughter of Jerusalem" is used in a lament (Lam. 2:15) and in an oracle of salvation (Isa. 52:1f.). "The daughter of my people . . . of Jerusalem . . . of Zion" appears in Lam. 2:11–13 (a lament), and "daughter of Zion . . . of Judah" occurs in Lam. 2:1–4 (also a lament). "Daughter of Zion . . . of my people" was used by Jeremiah in an oracle of woe (Jer. 6:22–26), while "daughter of Judah" appears in Lam. 1:15; 2:5, and in Ps. 97:8 (an oracle of hope). Other variations on the title are "daughter of my people" (Jer. 4:11; 8:18 to 9:1; Lam. 3:46–51; 4:3, 6, 10), and "daughter of my dispersed ones" which was used in an oracle of restoration (Zeph. 3:10).

The use of the title "daughter of Zion" and its variations seems to have begun with Isaiah ben Amoz (740–700 B.C.). The term "the virgin Israel" appeared slightly earlier in an oracle from Amos:

> Hear this word which I take up over you in lamentation,
> O house of Israel:

> "Fallen, no more to rise,
>   is the virgin Israel;
>   forsaken on her land,
>   with none to raise her up."
>   (Amos 5:1f.)

The Hebrew word here is $b^{e}thulah$ (as also in Jer. 18:13; 31:21; Lam. 2:10). The English word "virgin" is a precise translation. Thus this cluster of passages refers to the nation as a girl who had "not yet known a man."

Titles given Jerusalem or Israel also were applied to other nations. Both "daughter of Zion" and "the daughters of Moab" appear in Isa. 16:1f., cited earlier here. "The daughters of Moab" was applied to Moabite refugees seeking sanctuary in Jerusalem. When used of nations or peoples other than Israel, the idiom appeared often in predictions of woe. Thus an oracle against Babylon begins:

> Come down and sit in the dust,
>   O virgin daughter of Babylon;
>   sit on the ground without a throne,

> O daughter of the Chaldeans!
> For you shall no more be called
>   tender and delicate.
>
>   (Isa. 47:1)[75]

Other nations designated by the title were Egypt (Jer. 46:11f., 24), Moab (Isa. 15:2f.), Sidon (Isa. 23:12), Ammon (Jer. 49:1–5), and Edom (Lam. 4:21f.).

In an extensive series of passages usually predicting judgment, the land (or the city as the epitome of the land) is referred to as feminine even though the titles just discussed are absent. Often this is done in a way which appears in an English translation as a series of feminine pronouns. In some cases, the feminine pronouns might be held to refer back to an antecedent feminine noun, as in Ezek. 22:1–3 (where "city" is feminine in Hebrew). In other cases, however, the antecedent is masculine even though the personification is feminine. Jer. 5:9–11 is an example:

> Shall I not punish them for these things?
>   says the LORD;
>   and shall I not avenge myself
>   on a nation such as this?
> Go up through her vine-rows and destroy,
>   but make not a full end;
> strip away her branches,
>   for they are not the LORD's.
> For the house of Israel and the house of Judah
>   have been utterly faithless to me,
>   says the LORD.

She to whom the vine-rows and branches belong is "a nation such as this," and the word for nation is masculine in Hebrew.[76]

The authors of the Old Testament do not explain the significance of their feminine personification of the nation. The validity of modern psychological interpretations, which presuppose a transcultural validity for our categories of psychological analysis, has never been established. Thus Freudian or Jungian explanations are not demonstrable. We do know that the ancient Israelites used highly evocative figures and similes in their literature. It also is clear from the material we have just covered that the personification of the nation as a woman was used in statements of either great peril or great hope. It seems fair to conclude that feminine personifications may have been used because of the high standing of woman in Israel. Even though the male acted as the epitome of the family and nation in normal affairs, the female became the epitome of the whole people in times of great urgency.

III

Three feminine nouns are used in the Old Testament to describe some of the activity of God. The spirit *(ruach)* of God is virtually an hypostatization of God acting in the world; the wisdom *(chokmah)* of God is an hypostatization of God's purposes; and the righteousness of God appears in both a masculine *(tsedeq)* and a feminine *(ts^{e}daqah)* form. Statistically, the most important of these feminine nouns is spirit *(ruach)*, but it is the wisdom *(chokmah)* of God which is personified as a woman. It is difficult to determine the significance of the choice of gender in the use of the two forms of the word for righteousness.[77] We will restrict our discussion to the personifications of God's wisdom as a woman. We then will move to a consideration of the gender of Israel's name for God.

Wisdom appears as a female in five passages in the book of The Proverbs (1:20–33; 3:13–18; 4:3–13; 8:1–36; 9:1–6). The level of the personification varies. It is minimal in ch. 3:13–18 where the feminine personal pronoun takes the feminine noun *chokmah* (wisdom) as its anteced-ent. In ch. 9:1–6, however, Wisdom has become a wealthy woman, or possibly a fertility cult goddess:

> Wisdom has built her house,
>   she has set up her seven pillars.
> She has slaughtered her beasts, she has mixed her wine,
>   she has also set her table.
> She has sent out her maids to call
>   from the highest places in the town,
> "Whoever is simple, let him turn in here!"
>   To him who is without sense she says,
> "Come, eat of my bread
>   and drink of the wine I have mixed.
> Leave simpleness, and live,
>   and walk in the way of insight."

Except in ch. 9:1–6, just quoted, the instruction given by Wisdom is equated with a knowledge of the will of God. It is "the fear of the Lord" (ch. 1:29) or a knowl-edge of "the paths of uprightness" (ch. 4:11). "The words of [her] mouth are righteous" (ch. 8:8) because "the fear of the Lord is hatred of evil" (ch. 8:13). Thus Wisdom walks "in the way of righteousness, in the paths of justice" (ch. 8:20).

Wisdom is described in only two passages (excepting again ch. 9:1–6) in a way which makes it more than a synonym for the knowledge of the will of God.

> The Lord created me at the beginning of his work,
>   the first of his acts of old.
> Ages ago I was set up,
>   at the first, before the beginning of the earth.
> When there were no depths I was brought forth,
>   when there were no springs abounding with water.
> Before the mountains had been shaped,
>   before the hills, I was brought forth;

before he had made the earth with its fields,
  or the first of the dust of the world.
When he established the heavens, I was there,
  when he drew a circle on the face of the deep,
when he made firm the skies above,
  when he established the fountains of the deep,
when he assigned to the sea its limit,
  so that the waters might not transgress his command,
when he marked out the foundations of the earth,
  then I was beside him, like a master workman;
and I was daily his delight,
  rejoicing before him always,
rejoicing in his inhabited world
  and delighting in the sons of men.

(Prov. 8:22–31)

We are told in Prov. 3:19f. that

the LORD by wisdom founded the earth;
  by understanding he established the heavens;
by his knowledge the deeps broke forth,
  and the clouds drop down the dew.

If Prov. 3:19f. and ch. 8:22–31 be read together, Wisdom, created before the world and its inhabitants had been formed, becomes the artificer (ch. 8:30) assisting God in creating heavens and earth. If this figure be related to the Wisdom who instructs humanity, then the sages of ancient Israel believed that the orderly universe and the orderly life reflected the same divine will.

All the religions of Israel's neighbors were polytheistic, and their pantheons included deities that were male and female. Thus they expressed in their gods both the feminine and the masculine. There is little doubt that the sages responsible for the book of The Proverbs intended to create a feminine personification of the Wisdom of God. This, however, falls far short of the "feminine principle" incarnated in the Queen of Heaven, the great ancient Near Eastern goddess of fertility. A statement of what this may mean must be deferred until we have reviewed other relevant evidence.

The proper name for Israel's God is YHWH. It was so sacred and so powerful that it came to be pronounced only rarely. In the text of the Hebrew Bible, it was given the vowels for *'adonai* ("lord") so that it would be pronounced as *'adonai* when encountered in reading.

Even though this footnote to the history of the transmission of the Hebrew text is a tribute to the deep piety of Judaism, it also explains an odd problem in Biblical theology. If we had had preserved for us the vowels used when the name of God was pronounced, we might be able better to understand the name itself. Given only the consonants YHWH, we have to use more conjecture than is desirable.

A few statements about the proper name of God can be made with confidence. One is that it existed both as YHWH and as YH or YHW. We find the shorter forms both in personal names and in fifth-century B.C. documents from a colony of Jews living in Egypt at Elephantine. Joshua is *Y*^{*e*}*hoshua'* in Hebrew and probably means "Yah saves," while Josiah *(Yo'shiyahu)* means "Yahu supports."[78] The Elephantine Papyri give the name of God as Yahu (or Ya'u).[79]

Another kind of statement can be made about YHWH. The Hebrew verb has two tenses (completed and incomplete action) and six modes. One of the modes is causal. If the Hebrew verb for "to become" be put into the causal mode, it would probably become Yahweh in the third person masculine singular. It would mean "He causes to come into being." We have to say "probably" because no causal form of the verb "to become" occurs in the Old Testament (except, possibly, in the name of God itself). Thus we lack other examples of the causal mode of the verb "to become" with which to check our application of the rules for verb forms to this one verb.

Having both a long and a shorter form of the name, we seem to face the possibility that the original name was one of the shorter forms. Not being confident that the long form is a verb in the causal mode, we appear to be unable to identify the root from which it was taken and thus cannot determine its meaning. A final complication seems to exist in the suggestion that the final *H* in YHWH indicates that it is a feminine noun since many feminine nouns are formed by adding a final *h* to a root containing three other consonants.

Frank Moore Cross has clarified the problem. He has pointed out that the long form of the name, YHWH, appears in non-Biblical sources as far back as the eighth century B.C. (possibly as far back as the fourteenth). The oldest evidence for the shorter form, YHW, outside the Old Testament comes in material dated from the fifth century B.C. Thus YHWH, the long form, is very early.[80] Furthermore, Cross provides evidence of the use in the ancient Near East of the causal mode of the verb "to become" in deity names which were brief sentences such as "the God N——brings (or brought) into being (a child)."[81] These sentences appear to be statements traditionally made in a cultic context. Cross thus can write, "Our evidence also points strongly to the conclusion that *yahwê* is a shortened form of a sentence name taken from a cultic formula."[82]

I find this convincing. It identifies the name of Israel's God as the third person masculine singular Hiphil (causal mode) of the verb "to become." Two conclusions can be drawn from this. The first is that the ancient Israelites believed their god to be masculine. The second is that the Lord was so uniquely the Creator that "He creates" became the name of God. Is it possible that the absence of examples of the causal mode of the verb "to become" in the Old Testament is due to the absorption of all creative activity into God? Perhaps so, although it

is difficult to see how it could be either proven or dis-
proven.

IV

The materials discussed thus far in the examination of
the gender of the name of Israel's God have given an
unclear picture. The personification of the wisdom of
God was feminine and was described as a woman. The
name YHWH seems to be a masculine verbal form. Furthermore, words describing God's activity are both feminine (spirit) and masculine (word, glory), or either masculine or feminine (righteousness).

The evidence that should be considered in a discussion of the gender of the name of the God of Israel would
be incomplete without mention of the intense, sustained
polemic in the Old Testament against the female and
male gods of Israel's neighbors and of the earlier inhabitants of the land. All who are at all familiar with the Old
Testament, especially with the Deuteronomic literature
(Deuteronomy, Judges, Samuel, Kings) and the prophetic books, can document this statement for themselves.

A single example from Jeremiah will illustrate the
point:

> How can you say, "I am not defiled,
>   I have not gone after the Baals"?
> Look at your way in the valley;
>   know what you have done—
> a restive young camel interlacing her tracks,
>   a wild ass used to the wilderness,
> in her heat sniffing the wind!
>   Who can restrain her lust?
> None who seek her need weary themselves;
>   in her month they will find her.

> Keep your feet from going unshod
> and your throat from thirst.
> But you said, "It is hopeless,
> for I have loved strangers,
> and after them I will go."
>
> (Jer. 2:23–25)

Those who prefer a more explicit statement might read the description of the reformation of Josiah (II Kings 23:4–14). Baal and Ashteroth were the male and female gods respectively.

The strength of the Yahwist attack on religions which deified the feminine and masculine principles makes it extremely unlikely that the same thing was being done in Yahwism under another guise. Reading that into the masculine name of God and the female personification of God's wisdom is almost certainly wrong.

It seems likely that the ancient Israelites believed passionately that their God, the creator of all that was, transcended gender. Sexuality was a part of God's creation. Therefore it was intrinsically good. Nonetheless, it was part of the creation, not of the Creator who transcended the creation. The sexual functions of both female and male were sacred because they shared in the continuing creativity of God. Neither was divine in itself, nor were the two complete when joined together. New life came into being when female and male had been joined together, and when their union had been made fecund by the creative intervention of God. Without that divine intervention there was no new life.

Conclusion

This conclusion will summarize the findings of the preceding chapters. Each chapter has had a summary, but a more inclusive summary now is in order.

The God of ancient Israel was understood to be the creator, "He who caused to come into being." The Lord had created the world, had created a people by leading slaves out of bondage, and lived in the midst of that people to sustain and prosper them, or to punish and cleanse them.

The relationship between God and people was mediated by various offices in the cult, but it was actualized primarily by the appearance of new life within the people of God, by the ebb and flow of fecundity in nature, and by the varying fortunes of the people of God in relationship to the other peoples of the ancient world.

The new life given the people of God came into being because the Lord worked in the woman's womb, bringing to fruition the sexual relations of husband and wife. Thus the woman was uniquely the locus of the basic manifestation of the benign presence of God in the midst of the people, for without new life the people would soon cease to exist. This function of the woman, and the intimate and demanding nurture of the young that resulted from it, was so crucial that woman, its primary agent, was reinforced in many ways. She had the option of attending the major festivals rather than the obligation to go. She was guaranteed, as far as possible, the sexual access to her husband necessary to her role, and the economic security essential to its completion. Although she had access to communal affairs outside the home, her participation was voluntary rather than mandatory. Men, lacking so crucial a function, were assigned two roles: the epitome of the family, a position not normally held by a woman, and the priestly office, a position never held by a woman. The reinforcements given women should be understood in the context of a high death rate for mothers and infants in childbirth. The survival of the people always was in question. The conserving of the agent by which it was to be achieved was essential.

Those women who had outlived the age of childbearing, who had recognized abilities, or to whom the Lord appeared, seem to have functioned outside the home in all capacities except the priesthood. The number of the reports of such women is small. This is probably to be attributed to the death rate in childbirth and to the demands on energy and time made by child care and homemaking. There is no evidence that public careers were closed to women, or that they were felt to be unqualified to occupy them. On the contrary, there is ample evidence that women did function in a wide range of careers, from ruler to businesswoman, from prophetess to sage.

We must conclude, therefore, that the status of woman in the Old Testament is high. She is given the honor due to one in whom God acts directly and uniquely. She exercised full participation in the life of the community. Because the Old Testament is a God-centered literature, the role of woman is best stated as a doctrine. She was co-worker with God in the creating and sustaining of the people of God. She also participated fully and freely in the common life of that people.

Notes

1. Earle Bennett Cross, *The Hebrew Family: A Study in Historical Sociology* (The University of Chicago Press, 1927), p. 39.

2. Roland de Vaux, *Ancient Israel: Its Life and Institutions,* tr. by John McHugh (Toronto: McGraw-Hill Book Co. of Canada, Ltd., 1961), p. 20.

3. Anthony Phillips, "Some Aspects of Family Law in Pre-Exilic Israel," *Vetus Testamentum,* Vol. XXIII (1973), p. 350.

4. Ismar J. Peritz, "Women in the Ancient Hebrew Cult," *Journal of Biblical Literature,* Vol. XVII (1898), pp. 111–48. Circulated also as a reprint.

5. Clarence J. Vos, *Woman in Old Testament Worship* (Delft: Verenigde Drukkerijen Judels & Brinkman, n. d.).

6. Elizabeth Mary MacDonald, *The Position of Women as Reflected in Semitic Codes of Law* (Toronto: The University of Toronto Press, 1931).

7. Millar Burrows, *The Basis of Israelite Marriage* (American Oriental Society, 1938). Burrows' argument weakens the hypothesis that the father or husband owned the daughter or wife.

8. Phyllis Trible, "Depatriarchalizing in Biblical Interpretation," *Journal of the American Academy of Religion,* Vol. XLI (1973), pp. 30–47.

9. Such as Thomas Edward McComisky, *The Status of the Secondary Wife: Its Development in Ancient Near Eastern Law* (University Microfilm, 1970); Bernard F. Batto, *Studies on Women at Mari* (The Johns Hopkins University Press, 1974); Ilse Seibert, *Woman in the Ancient Near East,* tr. by Marianne Herzfeld (Leipzig: Edition Leipzig, 1974); and P. A. H. de Boer, *Fatherhood and Motherhood in Israelite and Judean Piety* (Leiden: E. J. Brill, 1974). The two last-named defend the traditional patriarchal interpretation. Seibert is sumptuously illustrated.

10. No single recent book describes all kinds of Biblical criticism. A series of booklets published by Fortress Press is useful: Norman C. Habel, *Literary Criticism of the Old Testament* (1971); Gene M. Tucker, *Form Criticism of the Old Testament* (1971); Walter E. Rast, *Tradition, History, and the Old Testament* (1972); and J. Maxwell Miller, *The Old Testament and the Historian* (1976). Ralph W. Klein, *Textual Criticism of the Old Testament: The Septuagint After Qumran* (1973), describes textual criticism.

11. Otto Eissfeldt, *The Old Testament: An Introduction,* tr. by Peter R. Ackroyd (Harper & Row, Publishers, Inc., 1965).

12. The Priestly source (P) is the latest of the four major strands that have been woven together to form the Pentateuch as we now have it. The authors of P seem to have written at the end of the exile while living in Babylonia. They thus probably knew this creation story in its Babylonian version. The Babylonian version, *The Enuma Elish*, describes the creation of humanity in these words:

> When Marduk hears the words of the gods,
> His heart prompts [him] to fashion artful works.
> Opening his mouth, he addresses Ea
> To impart the plan he has conceived in his heart:
> "Blood I will mass and cause bones to be.
> I will establish a savage, 'man' shall be his name.
> Verily, savage-man I will create.
> He shall be charged with the service of the gods,
>   that they might be at ease!"

E. A. Speiser, "Akkadian Myths and Epics," in James B. Pritchard (ed.), *Ancient Near Eastern Texts Relating to the Old Testament*, 2d ed. (Princeton University Press, 1955), p. 69c. Humanity is created to be the slaves of the gods in *The Enuma Elish*.

13. Gerhard von Rad, *Genesis, A Commentary*, tr. by John H. Marks, The Old Testament Library (The Westminster Press, 1961), pp. 56f. Cited hereafter as *Genesis*.

14. *Ibid.*, p. 81.

15. The verb in the final clause of Gen. 3:16 *(m sh l)* has been taken to mean "to rule," at least since the time of the Septuagint, a Greek translation from about 200 B.C. The root *m sh l*, however, can also mean "to liken." The object of the verb in this verse is governed by a preposition difficult to relate to the meaning "to rule"

but easy to relate to "to liken." The root *m sh l* elsewhere in the Hebrew Old Testament is not translated "to liken" in the mode used here. The translation given in RSV, NEB, etc., is traditional. An *n* would have to be prefixed to the root before it could be translated "to be like." Were this done, the line would read, "and he [your husband] shall be like you."

16. The phrase "and many concubines" is lacking in NEB, which carries the notation that the Hebrew here preserves two unintelligible words. *The Jerusalem Bible,* ed. by Alexander Jones (Doubleday & Company, Inc., 1966), translates "and every human luxury, chest on chest of it," giving the obscure word its post-Biblical meaning.

17. William McKane, *Proverbs, A New Approach,* The Old Testament Library (The Westminster Press, 1970), p. 658. Cited hereafter as *Proverbs.*

18. Louis M. Epstein, *Marriage Laws in the Bible and the Talmud* (Harvard University Press, 1942), p. 38, n. 17, cites Gen. 35: 22 and II Sam. 3:8 for other examples of this, and sec. 158 of the Code of Hammurabi for a Babylonian parallel.

19. "If a Man," secs. 28 to 30 in Ephraim Neufeld, *The Hittite Laws: Translated Into English and Hebrew with a Commentary* (London: Luzac & Company, Inc., 1951), pp. 8f., for Hittite laws regulating payments of the "bride price."

20. H. Wheeler Robinson, "The Hebrew Conception of Corporate Personality," in P. Volz, F. Stummer, and J. Hempel (eds.), *Werden und Wesen des Alten Testaments: Vorträge gehalten auf der internationalen Tagung alttestament-*

licher Forschung zu Göttingen vom 4.–10. September 1935. (Berlin: Alfred Töpelmann, 1936), pp. 49–62.

21. Burrows, *op. cit.,* p. 12. For a different interpretation, see Johannes Pedersen, *Israel: Its Life and Culture* (Copenhagen: Povl Branner, Pts. I–II, 1926; Pts. III–IV, 1940), Pts. I–II, p. 68. Cited hereafter as Pedersen, *Israel I–II,* or *Israel III–IV.*

22. Pedersen, *Israel I–II,* p. 70.

23. David R. Mace, *Hebrew Marriage: A Sociological Study* (Philosophical Library, Inc., 1953), p. 122.

24. So, among others, de Vaux, *op. cit.,* pp. 25f.; Mace, *op. cit.,* p. 129.

25. De Vaux, *op. cit.,* p. 40.

26. A concubine is a slave who had become a wife. She had rights but was inferior to the wife who was an Israelite freewoman. See McComisky, *op. cit.,* pp. 20–50, for a survey of the legal status of the concubine throughout the ancient Near East.

27. The earliest stratum (J) records the genealogical promise in Gen. 12:2f.; 13:14–17 (where it is linked with the promise of a land); 15:5. E (the second oldest stratum) reports the promise in Gen. 17:17–19. It then appears in P (the latest stratum) in Gen. 17:1–8.

28. RSV margin, a more difficult but perhaps more literal translation. NEB: "You do not know how a pregnant woman comes to have a body and a living spirit in her womb."

29. See Gen. 18:9–15; 29:31–35; 30:1–8, 17f., 22, for similar reports about the wives of other patriarchs.

30. Pedersen, *Israel III–IV,* p. 300. Parenthetical insert is mine.

31. See Chapter 4 and such passages as Josh. 15:16f. (Judg. 1:11f.); Judg. 21:1–23; I Sam. 18:17–28; Jer. 29:6.

32. Jer. 3:24. Explicit references to daughters and sons in references to punishment occur often. See Josh. 7:16–25; Jer. 11:22; 48:46; Lam. 1:18; 5:11; Ezek. 24: 21–25; Joel 3:8; Amos 7:16f.; 8:13f. Jer. 48:46 and Joel 3:8 are directed against Moab and Phoenicia respectively.

33. E.g.: Noah—Gen. 6:18; 7:13; 8:16, 18; Abram, Abraham—Gen. 12:5; 13:1; etc.; Lot—Gen. 14:16; Esau —Gen. 36:6.

34. As a verb: Gen. 20:3; Deut. 21:13; 22:22; 24:1; Isa. 54:1, 5; 62:4f.; Jer. 3:14; 31:32 (but note ASV margin, "I was lord over them"). As a noun: Gen. 20:3; Ex. 21:3, 22; Deut. 22:22; 24:4; II Sam. 11:26; Joel 1:8; Prov. 12:4; 31:11, 23, 28; Esth. 1:17, 20.

35. As Friedrich Nötscher has put it: "The realm of the wife is the home. She is the mother of the husband's children, but *more as servant than companion."* (*Biblische Altertumskunde* [Bonn: Peter Hanstein, 1940], p. 81. Italics are Nötscher's.) He added, however, "The legal and actual place of the wife in respect to the man in biblical times is, after all, not easily described" *(loc. cit.).* De Vaux, *op. cit.,* p. 39, adding that the wife also addressed the husband as *'adon* in Gen. 18:12; Judg. 19:26; Amos

4:1, held that "she addressed him, in fact, as a slave addressed his master, or a subject his king." Pedersen, *Israel I–II*, pp. 62f., described the baal-husband as the "ruling will" within the family.

36. See C. F. Burney, *The Book of Judges, with Introduction and Notes,* 2d ed. (London: Rivington's, 1930), pp. 444f., where the similarities are given in detail.

37. See a report of a trial by ordeal for murder in Austin Kennett, *Bedouin Justice: Laws and Customs Among the Egyptian Bedouin* (Cambridge: Cambridge University Press, 1925), pp. 107–114. The incident is reported more briefly by R. H. Kennett, Austin Kennett's father, in *Ancient Hebrew Social Life and Custom as Indicated in Law, Narrative, and Metaphor* (London: Humphrey Milford, 1933), pp. 95–97.

38. So, among others, Georg Beer, *Die soziale und religiöse Stellung der Frau im israelitischen Altertum* (Tübingen: J. C. B. Mohr, 1919), p. 16.

39. Raphael Loewe, *The Position of Women in Judaism* (London: S.P.C.K., 1966), p. 45, writes: "It is significant that the Hebrew expression for 'officiant' at a service means literally 'agent of a group.' Priesthood, as a matter of spiritual status as understood in the Christian West, is a category foreign to Judaism." This is difficult to reconcile with language used of Levitical and Aaronic priests in the Old Testament, but it does have the sense of corporate identification necessary for any individual or group in the Old Testament.

40. References in the Old Testament to Hittites are an example of this. The existence of the Hittites was questioned by historians because of the silence of other an-

cient sources. Now we know enough about them to quote from their laws because archaeologists have recovered extensive remains from their culture.

41. Batto, *op. cit.,* pp. 8–21, describes the great power exercised by Shibtu, the wife of Zimri-Lim, king of Mari and a contemporary of Hammurabi. I know of no equivalent description of the power of the queen mother in the ancient Near East, although it may well exist.

42. The fragmentary condition of a Hittite law dealing with the relationship between mother and son gives an intriguing but ambiguous impression: "If a mother casts out the garments of her son, she expels her son; if her son comes back and takes his door and throws it out [side] he takes his . . . and his . . . and casts them out, then she may take them back, and her son shall become her son once more." ("If a Vine," sec. 171 in Neufeld, *op. cit.,* p. 47.) The precise meaning of this passage is best left to the imagination. It is to be hoped that each Hittite house was surrounded by ample open space! The Old Testament makes no provision for disowning a child.

43. For a brief discussion of the problems, see McKane, *Proverbs,* p. 408.

44. Code of Hammurabi, secs. 146, 147. G. R. Driver and John C. Miles, *The Babylonian Laws, Edited with Translation and Commentary,* 2 vols. (Oxford: Clarendon Press, 1952, 1955), Vol. II, p. 57.

45. De Vaux, *op. cit.,* pp. 144–46; Eissfeldt, *op. cit.,* pp. 27–29.

46. This explanation is offered by Von Rad, *Genesis,* p. 187, and E. A. Speiser, *Genesis, Translated with an Introduc-*

tion and Notes, The Anchor Bible (Doubleday & Company, Inc., 1964), p. 117.

47. Passages reporting the domination of husband by wife have been dismissed by some scholars. Ecclesiasticus (Sirach) 25:16–18 is such a passage:

> I would rather dwell with a lion and a dragon
>> than dwell with an evil wife.
> The wickedness of a wife changes her appearance,
>> and darkens her face like that of a bear.
> Her husband takes his meals among the neighbors,
>> and he cannot help sighing bitterly.

George Beer wrote that these lines suggest that the husband often was "*de facto* the slave of a lawless wife" (*op. cit.*, p. 24). Ecclesiasticus is one of the writings in the Roman Catholic canon assigned to the Apocrypha by Protestants.

48. Pedersen, *Israel I–II*, p. 69.

49. For slightly different statistics, see Peritz, *op. cit.*, pp. 130f., n. 36; Vos, *op. cit.*, p. 161. The pun implied in Gen. 4:1 indicates that Eve named Cain. If this interpretation stands, we have one more instance of a mother naming a child.

50. The presence of historical memories behind the story is widely recognized. Hermann Gunkel, *Genesis übersetzt und erklärt*(Göttingen: Vandenhoeck & Ruprecht, 1901), p. 337, calls it a historical saga telling of an incident involving the city of Shechem and three Israelite tribes, Dinah, Simeon, and Levi. The first merged with Shechem; the second and third attacked Shechem but were defeated by a coalition of Canaanites. For variations

(at times major) on this, see Von Rad, *Genesis,* pp. 329f., and Speiser, *Genesis,* pp. 266f.

51. See James Luther Mays, *Hosea, A Commentary,* The Old Testament Library (The Westminster Press, 1969), pp. 22–24. See pp. 24–60 for a review of various interpretations of Hos., chs. 1 to 3.

52. So Phillips, *op. cit.,* p. 352; de Vaux, *op. cit.,* p. 35.

53. As in W. P. Patterson, "Marriage," in James Hastings *et al.* (eds.) *A Dictionary of the Bible* (Charles Scribner's Sons, 1906), Vol. III, p. 274c. Paterson argued that the primitive freedom of the husband was later restricted by prophetic protest and the legislation derived from the protest. Phillips, *op. cit.,* p. 355, argues that Deut. 24:1 gave the husband virtually unrestricted rights of divorce. This legislation, at least in its present form, is usually dated about 650 B.C.

54. It needs also to be added that a husband's sexual faithlessness is described by the prophets as faithlessness to God. See Hos. 4:12–14; Jer. 5:7–9; Ezek. 18:10–13 as examples.

55. Although de Vaux, *op. cit.,* p. 35, reports that women in the Jewish colony at Elephantine could divorce their husbands (fifth to sixth centuries B.C.) and that an instance is reported from Judah in the second century A.D.

56. G. Ernest Wright, "The Book of Deuteronomy: Introduction and Exegesis," in G. A. Buttrick *et al.* (eds.), *The Interpreter's Bible* (Abingdon-Cokesbury Press, 1953), Vol. II, pp. 473f.

57. Gerhard von Rad, *Deuteronomy, A Commentary,* tr. by Dorothea Barton, The Old Testament Library (The Westminster Press, 1966), p. 150.

58. Mace, *op. cit.,* p. 258. The Code of Hammurabi, sec. 142, explicitly gave a wife the right to divorce her husband "if she has kept herself chaste and has no fault, while her husband is given to going about" (Driver and Miles, *op. cit.,* p. 57).

59. Chayim Cohen, "Widow," in Cecil Roth and Geoffrey Wigoder (eds.), *Encyclopedia Judaica* (Jerusalem: Kefer Publishing House, 1971), Vol. XVI, p. 487.

60. And by such later Jewish practices as those described by Louis M. Epstein, *Sex Laws and Customs in Judaism* (Ktav Publishing House, Inc., 1948, 1967), pp. 68–75.

61. In evaluating the role of Jezebel, John Gray, *I & II Kings, A Commentary,* 2d, fully rev., ed., The Old Testament Library (The Westminster Press, 1970), p. 435, reports: "Fohrer assumes that the centrality of Jezebel does not quite correspond to historical fact, but rather reflects the intense hatred of prophetic circles which transmitted the tradition. For her to contrive the judicial murder of Naboth within the letter of Hebrew law, she would have been, Fohrer declares, 'a world's wonder of learning and resource.' " But one of the points of the story is that she subverted the law.

62. Mace, *op. cit.,* p. 87.

63. Beer, *op. cit.,* pp. 34f.

64. As by Vos, *op. cit.*, p. 193: Only men supported families and the priesthood provided an income; some priestly duties required a male's strength; a mother was preoccupied with maternal duties; a woman became unclean periodically; and restricting the priesthood to one sex would discourage the intrusion of baalistic fertility worship practices. All are conjectures.

65. Vos, *op. cit.*, p. 186, describes Huldah as "a relatively unknown figure in Israel's history," although he adds: "In this period of Israel's history there was little if any prejudice against a woman's uttering a prophecy. If she had received the gift of prophecy, her words were to be given the same authority as those of a man."

66. Walther Eichrodt, *Ezekiel, A Commentary*, tr. by Cosslett Quin, The Old Testament Library (The Westminster Press, 1970), p. 169.

67. The Lord's visit to Abraham and Sarah (Gen. 18: 1–15) is a theophany in which Sarah shared. It is not discussed here. The theophany to Samson's mother in which her husband shared (Judg. 13:2–25) will be discussed.

68. Peritz, *op. cit.*, pp. 122f., adds two other examples: Judg. 21:6–25 and II Kings 4:23.

69. Vos, *op. cit.*, p. 79.

70. M. R. H. Löhr, *Die Stellung des Weibes zu Jahwereligion und -kult untersucht* (Leipzig: Hinrichs', 1908), pp. 38f.

71. See also Hos. 4:13f.; Jer. 7:17f.; 44:7–10, 15–27; Deut. 17:2–5; 29:18f.; II Chron. 15:13.

72. Martin Noth, *Leviticus, A Commentary*, tr. by J. E. Anderson, The Old Testament Library (The Westminster Press, 1965), p. 97.

73. So Vos, *op. cit.*, pp. 103, 129. For the traditional view, see R. S. Peake, "Unclean, Uncleanness," in James Hastings *et al.* (eds.), *A Dictionary of the Bible* (Charles Scribner's Sons, 1902), Vol. IV, p. 827.

74. The other oracles in this category are Micah 4:8 and Zeph. 3:14–20, both late.

75. See also Ps. 137:8f.; Jer. 50:41–43; 51:27–33; Zech. 2:7.

76. The prevalence of the personification of a city, people, or nation as a woman other than a daughter can be seen from the following:

Jerusalem: Ezek. 22:1–3; 24:6–9; Zeph. 3:1–7; Isa. 62:1–5

Zion: Lam. 1:17

Judah: Jer. 12:7–9; Ezek. 22:23–27

This nation (Israel and Judah): Jer. 5:7–11

The enemy: Micah 7:8–10

Assyria: Ezek. 32:22f.; Zeph. 2:13–15

Babylon or Chaldea: Jer. 50:8–16, 24–27, 29f., 35–38, 39f., 44–46; 51:1–5, 6–10, 36f., 45–49, 52f., 54–58

Egypt or Thebes: Ezek. 32:18–20; Nahum 3:8–13

Edom: Ezek. 32:29

Elam: Ezek. 32:24f.

Tyre: Ezek. 26:4–8; Zech. 9:3f.

Sidon: Ezek. 28:20–23

All such passages may not be included.

77. The masculine form is the more widely used. The feminine form appears in Ps. 36:6; 71:19; 99:4; Isa. 1:27; 5:16; 28:17; Jer. 9:24; Job 37:23; Dan. 9:7; Micah 7:9 (translated as "deliverance" in RSV). It is difficult to believe that there was no significance in the choice of the one form over the other, although the reason may have merely been euphemy.

78. A list of names compounded with Yah and Yahu is given in G. Buchanan Gray, *Studies in Hebrew Proper Names* (London: Adam and Charles Black, 1890), App. 113A, 113B, pp. 281–300. See pp. 149–63 for his discussion.

79. A. Cowley, *Aramaic Papyri of the Fifth Century* B.C. (Oxford: Clarendon Press, 1923). As examples, see papyrus no. 6 (pp. 16f. for translation); and no. 30 (pp. 113f. for translation).

80. Frank Moore Cross, *Canaanite Myth and Hebrew Epic: Essays in the History of the Religion of Israel* (Harvard University Press, 1973), pp. 61f. See Walther Eichrodt, *Theology of the Old Testament,* tr. by J. A. Baker, The Old Testament Library (The Westminster Press, 1961), Vol. I, pp. 187–94, for a discussion of this debate.

81. Cross, *op. cit.,* pp. 62–66.

82. *Ibid.,* p. 66.

Bibliography

Bible Texts and Versions

Biblia Hebraica, ed. by Rudolf Kittel, 3d ed. Stuttgart: Privilegierte Württembergische Bibelanstalt, 1937.

The Holy Bible. American Standard Version. Thomas Nelson & Sons, 1901.

The Holy Scriptures According to the Masoretic Text: A New Translation. The Jewish Publication Society of America, 1917.

The Jerusalem Bible, ed. by Alexander Jones. Doubleday & Company, Inc., 1966.

The New English Bible. Oxford University Press and Cambridge University Press, 1970. Available also in an *Oxford Study Edition,* ed. by Samuel Sandmel, M. Jack Suggs, and Arnold J. Tkacik. Oxford University Press, 1976.

The New Oxford Annotated Bible, ed. by Herbert G. May and Bruce M. Metzger. Oxford University Press, 1973.

General Works

Batto, Bernard Frank, *Studies on Women at Mari.* The Johns Hopkins University Press, 1974.

Beer, Georg, *Die soziale und religiöse Stellung der Frau im israelitischen Altertum.* Tübingen: J. C. B. Mohr, 1919.

de Boer, P. A. H., *Fatherhood and Motherhood in Israelite and Judean Piety.* Leiden: E. J. Brill, 1974.

Burney, C. F., *The Book of Judges, With Introduction and Notes,* 2d ed. London: Rivington's, 1930.

Burrows, Millar, *The Basis of Israelite Marriage.* American Oriental Society, 1938.

Cohen, Chayim, "Widow," in Cecil Roth and Geoffrey Wigoder (eds.), *Encyclopedia Judaica.* Jerusalem: Kefer Publishing House, 1971. Vol. XVI, pp. 487–95.

Cowley, A., *Aramaic Papyri of the Fifth Century* B.C. Oxford: Clarendon Press, 1923.

Cross, Earle Bennett, *The Hebrew Family: A Study in Historical Sociology.* The University of Chicago Press, 1927.

Cross, Frank Moore, *Canaanite Myth and Hebrew Epic: Essays in the History of the Religion of Israel.* Harvard University Press, 1973.

Driver, G. R., and Miles, John C., *The Babylonian Laws, Edited with Translation and Commentary,* 2 vols. Oxford: Clarendon Press, 1952, 1955.

Eichrodt, Walther, *Ezekiel, A Commentary,* tr. by Cosslett Quin. The Old Testament Library. The Westminster Press, 1970.

———*Theology of the Old Testament,* Vol. I, tr. by J. A. Baker. The Old Testament Library. The Westminster Press, 1961.

Eissfeldt, Otto, *The Old Testament: An Introduction,* tr. by Peter R. Ackroyd. Harper & Row, Publishers, Inc., 1965.

Epstein, Louis M., *Marriage Laws in the Bible and the Talmud.* Harvard University Press, 1942.

———*Sex Laws and Customs in Judaism.* Ktav Publishing House, Inc., 1948, 1967.

Gray, G. Buchanan, *Studies in Hebrew Proper Names.* London: Adam and Charles Black, 1890.

Gray, John, *I & II Kings, A Commentary,* 2d, fully rev., ed. The Old Testament Library. The Westminster Press, 1970.

Gunkel, Hermann, *Genesis übersetzt und erklärt.* Göttingen: Vandenhoeck & Ruprecht, 1901.

Habel, Norman C., *Literary Criticism of the Old Testament.* Fortress Press, 1971.

Kennett, Austin, *Bedouin Justice: Laws and Customs Among the Egyptian Bedouin.* Cambridge: Cambridge University Press, 1925.

Kennett, R. H., *Ancient Hebrew Social Life and Custom as Indicated* in *Law, Narrative, and Metaphor.* London: Humphrey Milford, 1933.

Klein, Ralph W., *Textual Criticism of the Old Testament: The Septuagint After Qumran.* Fortress Press, 1973.

Knierim, Rolf, "The Role of the Sexes in the Old Testament," *Lexington Theological Quarterly,* Vol. X, No. 4 (1975), pp. 2–10.

Löhr, M. R. H., *Die Stellung des Weibes zu Jahwe-religion und -kult untersucht.* Leipzig: Hinrichs', 1908.

Loewe, Raphael, *The Position of Women in Judaism.* London: S.P.C.K., 1966.

McComisky, Thomas Edward, *The Status of the Secondary Wife: Its Development in Ancient Near Eastern Law.* University Microfilm, 1970.

MacDonald, Elizabeth Mary, *The Position of Women as Reflected in Semitic Codes of Law.* Toronto: The University of Toronto Press, 1931.

McKane, William, *Proverbs, A New Approach.* The Old Testament Library. The Westminster Press, 1970.

Mace, David R., *Hebrew Marriage: A Sociological Study.* Philosophical Library, Inc., 1953.

Mays, James Luther, *Hosea, A Commentary.* The Old Testament Library. The Westminster Press, 1969.

Miller, J. Maxwell, *The Old Testament and the Historian.* Fortress Press, 1976.

Neufeld, Ephraim, *The Hittite Laws: Translated Into English and Hebrew with a Commentary.* London: Luzac & Company, Ltd., 1951.

Nötscher, Friedrich, *Biblische Altertumskunde.* Bonn: Peter Hanstein, 1940.

Noth, Martin, *Leviticus, A Commentary,* tr. by J. E. Anderson. The Old Testament Library. The Westminster Press, 1965.

Patterson, W. P., "Marriage," in James Hastings *et al.* (eds.), *A Dictionary of the Bible.* Charles Scribner's Sons, 1906. Vol. III, pp. 262–77.

Peake, A.S., "Unclean, Uncleanness," in James Hastings *et al.* (eds.), *A Dictionary of the Bible.* Charles Scribner's Sons, 1902. Vol. IV, pp. 825–34.

Pedersen, Johannes, *Israel: Its Life and Culture.* Copenhagen: Povl Branner, Pts. I–II, 1926; Pts. III–IV, 1940.

Peritz, Ismar J., "Women in the Ancient Hebrew Cult," *Journal of Biblical Literature*, Vol. XVII, No. 2 (1898), pp. 111–48.

Phillips, Anthony, "Some Aspects of Family Law in Pre-Exilic Israel," *Vetus Testamentum*, Vol. XXIII, fasc. 3 (1973), pp. 349–61.

von Rad, Gerhard, *Deuteronomy, A Commentary*, tr. by Dorothea Barton. The Old Testament Library. The Westminster Press, 1966.

——*Genesis, A Commentary*, tr. by John H. Marks. The Old Testament Library. The Westminster Press, 1961.

Rast, Walter E., *Tradition History and the Old Testament*. Fortress Press, 1972.

Robinson, H. Wheeler, "The Hebrew Conception of Corporate Personality," in *Werden und Wesen des Alten Testaments. Vorträge gehalten auf der internationalen Tagung alttestamentlicher Forschung zu Göttingen vom 4.–10. September 1935*, ed. by P. Volz, F. Stummer, and J. Hempel. Berlin: Alfred Töpelmann, 1936.

Seibert, Ilse, *Woman in Ancient Near East*, tr. by Marianne Herzfeld. Leipzig: Edition Leipzig, 1974.

Speiser, E. A., "Akkadian Myths and Epics," in James B. Pritchard (ed.), *Ancient Near Eastern Texts Relating to the Old Testament*, 2d ed. Princeton University Press, 1955.

——*Genesis: Translated with Introduction and Notes*, The Anchor Bible. Doubleday & Company, Inc., 1964.

Trible, Phyllis, "Depatriarchalizing in Biblical Interpretation," *Journal of the American Academy of Religion*, Vol. XLI, No. 1 (1973), pp. 30–47.

Tucker, Gene M., *Form Criticism of the Old Testament*. Fortress Press, 1971.

de Vaux, Roland, *Ancient Israel: Its Life and Institutions*, tr. by John McHugh. Toronto: McGraw-Hill Book Co. of Canada, Ltd., 1961.

Vos, Clarence J., *Woman in Old Testament Worship*. Delft: Verenigde Drukkerijen Judels & Brinkman, n.d.

Wright, G. Ernest, "The Book of Deuteronomy: Introduction and Exegesis," in *The Interpreter's Bible*, ed. by G. A. Buttrick *et al.* Abingdon-Cokesbury Press, 1953. Vol. II, pp. 311–537.

Index
of Biblical Passages

213